BLUEPRINTS

The Primary Assembly Book 1

Terry Gilbert

Stanley Thornes (Publishers) Ltd

Do you receive **BLUEPRINTS NEWS?**

Blueprints is an expanding series of practical teacher's ideas books and photocopiable resources for use in primary schools. Books are available for separate infant and junior age ranges for every core and foundation subject, as well as for an ever widening range of other primary teaching needs. These include **Blueprints Primary English** books and **Blueprints Resource Banks**. **Blueprints** are carefully structured around the demands of the National Curriculum in England and Wales, but are used successfully by schools and teachers in Scotland, Northern Ireland and elsewhere.

Blueprints provide:

- *Total curriculum coverage*
- *Hundreds of practical ideas*
- *Books specifically for the age range you teach*
- *Flexible resources for the whole school or for individual teachers*
- *Excellent photocopiable sheets – ideal for assessment and children's work profiles*
- *Supreme value.*

Books may be bought by credit card over the telephone and information obtained on **(01242) 577944**. Alternatively, photocopy and return this **FREEPOST** form to receive **Blueprints News**, our regular update on all new and existing titles. You may also like to add the name of a friend who would be interested in being on the mailing list.

Please add my name to the **BLUEPRINTS NEWS** mailing list.

Mr/Mrs/Miss/Ms _____

Home address _____

_____ Postcode _____

School address _____

_____ Postcode _____

Please also send **BLUEPRINTS NEWS** to:

Mr/Mrs/Miss/Ms _____

Address _____

_____ Postcode _____

To: Marketing Services Dept., Stanley Thornes Ltd, FREEPOST (GR 782), Cheltenham, GL50 1BR

Text © Terry Gilbert 1996

Original line illustrations by Pat Murray © ST(P) Ltd 1996

The right of Terry Gilbert to be identified as author of this work has been asserted by him in accordance with the Copyright, Designs and Patents Act 1988.

First published in 1996 by:
Stanley Thornes (Publishers) Ltd
Ellenborough House
Wellington Street
CHELTENHAM GL50 1YW

A catalogue record for this book is available from the British Library.

ISBN 0 7487 2614 4

96 97 98 99 00 / 10 9 8 7 6 5 4 3 2 1

Typeset by Tech-Set, Gateshead, Tyne and Wear
Printed and bound in Great Britain

CONTENTS

AUTHOR'S PREFACE

I believe assemblies should be about enthusiasm, love, wonder and interest. They should be vital, sincere and dignified with an emphasis always on inviting rather than compelling. Each person present at an assembly will take away that which is significant to him/her at that time.

Teachers know that all children love to watch other children performing or participating; that most children love to participate themselves and that some need to be encouraged to take part. Opportunities in school assembly should be given for children to share their experiences and tell about what is important to them. The talents of staff and pupils should be used together in order to celebrate the values of the school community.

Children must be interested if their spirits are to be roused and, no doubt, all will agree that careful preparation and the use of material that is relevant and stimulating will result in inspiring assemblies for all concerned. It is hoped that the material presented in this book will provide the ideas for users to produce memorable assemblies of true worth and quality.

ABOUT THIS BOOK

This book contains thirty complete assemblies suitable for use in primary, junior and middle schools. All the assemblies have been used successfully in several different types of school. Each assembly is complete in itself and may be presented by an individual, group or class. The content of each assembly is easily photocopiable so that participants may be given various parts to read or learn.

The assemblies are deliberately simple in structure but their content may be extended if desired, and material is suggested which may be used to 'fill out' each assembly if required. The format of the assemblies is quite traditional and straightforward because most children feel comfortable and secure with the familiar.

The assemblies have been planned to require the minimum of preparation, but, again, each assembly is capable of 'extension' to involve greater variety of presentation and involvement. The Bible reference sections provide background material or Bible readings which may be included if desired. Most of the hymns which are suggested are from the BBC book *Come and Praise* but, naturally, others suitable for the themes may be substituted.

In line with Government guidelines, the assemblies are 'broadly Christian in character'.

ACKNOWLEDGEMENTS

The author and publishers wish to thank the following who have kindly given permission for the use of copyright material:

Pitman Publishing for 'The Flowers of Remembrance' from *A Calendar of Stories* by Lilian McCrea; Thomas Nelson and Sons Ltd. and Sylvia Brimer for use of adapted stories 'Peace', 'Hands' and 'Skilled Hands' from *A Morning Assembly Book*; James Clark & Co., Ltd., The Lutterworth Press for adapted stories 'Moony's Sandals' and 'Johnny's Missing' from *The Light and the Dark* by Ursula Wolfel; Chansitor Publications Ltd. and Betty Patston for use of adapted stories 'Why Summer Days are Longer', 'The House with the Golden Windows' 'The Miller, the Son and the Donkey' and 'The Man Who Sold His Shadow' from *Assemblies for the Primaries* by A. G. Patston; Quaker Home Service for adapted use of the story 'The Great Spirit speaks to a chief' from L.Violet Hodgkin's *A Book of Quaker Saints*; the poem 'The Quarrel' by Eleanor Farjeon from her book *Silver, Sand and Snow* published by Michael Joseph reprinted by permission of David Higham Associates; Chansitor Publications Ltd. for two poems from *Sing Praises* by J.M. MacDougall Ferguson published by Religious Education Press; for the verse 'Bread' from 'Bread, Wine and Gentleness' reproduced from *Flowing Streams* with the permission of the National Christian Education Council.

Every effort has been made to trace all the copyright holders, but if any have been overlooked, the publishers will be pleased to make the necessary arrangements at the first opportunity.

NEW YEAR

Opening music
As the children enter, music should be played by a pianist, group, orchestra or from a recording.

GREETING

Leader: 'I sincerely wish you all a happy and successful New Year. Good morning children.'

Children: 'Good morning (leader's name); good morning everyone.'
All adults present: 'Good morning children.'

INTRODUCTION

Welcome back to school after the Christmas holidays. No doubt you are all delighted to be back! I hope and trust you all received the Christmas presents you deserved!

Who would like to tell us about the best present(s) he/she received? (Invite a few children to describe their Christmas presents.)

Now we start a New Year and a new term. As our first joint act together, let us pray.

PRAYER

Dear God, we thank you for the joys of the Christmas holidays; we look forward to the rich promise that this New Year brings. Please be with us in our school and in our homes, in our work and in our play, throughout the year. Please bless our families and our friends, and please bless us.
Amen.

Hymn
The journey of life (*Come and Praise* 45).
Travel on, travel on (*Come and Praise* 42).

CONTENT

January, as you know, is the first month of the New Year. January was named after the Roman god, Janus. The word 'janitor' which means 'door-keeper' also comes from Janus. The god Janus was like a door-keeper, guarding the door to the New Year.

Janus was a very strange looking god because he had two faces. Can you imagine what it must be like to have two faces? Imagine having to clean two sets of teeth instead of one set twice a day! You see, Janus had two faces so that he was able to look forward and backward at the same time.

He was the god who was supposed to have all doors and entrances under his protection, and that is why he always carried a very large bunch of keys. One of these keys he used to unlock the door at the end of the year to enable the New Year to enter.

Hymn
One more step along the world I go (*Come and Praise* 47).
Father, lead me day by day.

CONTENT

I wonder what this New Year will bring?

No doubt the first snowdrops will soon appear with the promise of Spring. Presumably we shall welcome the Spring with its new life and Summer with its holiday joys. Autumn colour and fruits should follow and then winter will re-appear and we shall be giving and receiving Christmas presents again.

The seasons seem fixed, but other events will occur which we cannot predict. Some no doubt will be happy but others may be sad.

No matter what this New Year has in store, Christians believe that God will help and support us — and share in sad as well as happy times.

Let us end this assembly by closing our eyes and quietly listening to some words written by Louise Haskins and read by King George VIth in his Christmas Day broadcast to the nation in 1939.

CLOSING PRAYER — READING

'And I said to the man who stood at the gate of the year: Give me a light that I may tread safely into the unknown. And he replied: Go out into the darkness and put your hand into the hand of God. That shall be to you better than light and safer than a known way.'

Closing music
A few bars of music, played quietly by the pianist.
Any necessary announcements.

Recessional music
Children leave accompanied by appropriate music played by pianist, group, orchestra or from a recording.

For younger children
(For involvement before, during or after assembly.)

- Tell about Christmas presents received.

- Write or tell about things they would like to happen during the New Year.

- Paint a picture of Janus (the Roman God with two faces).

For older children
(For involvement before, during or after assembly.)

- Discuss 'New Year Resolutions' then write or tell about those they may wish to make.

- Find, read out (possibly write out for handwriting practice) and possibly learn by heart the poem called 'The Months' by Sara Coleridge.

- Illustrate the poem 'The Months' or paint a picture of Janus the two-faced Roman god.

Other New Year festivals and customs

- Rosh Hashanah is the first day of the Jewish New Year. It is on the first day of the Jewish month, Tishri (September–October).

- Diwali is the name given by Hindus to their New Year Festival. It is The Festival of Lights (October–November).

- The Chinese New Year celebrations last two weeks and usually begin any day between 21 January and 19 February (that is, the 23rd day of the 12th moon). On the third day of the festival the Lion Dance and Feast of Lanterns are held.

- Hogmanay is the Scottish name for New Year's Eve, 31 December. Scottish people celebrate the New Year with a party and they also observe important traditions during the Hogmanay folk festival celebrations.

- Japanese people begin preparing on 13 December for their 1 January New Year celebrations. They too observe important traditions during their six day festival.

THE FIVE SENSES

Opening music
Appropriate music is played (by pianist, school orchestra, group or recording) as children enter and take their places, quietly.

GREETING

Leader: 'Good morning children.'

Children: 'Good morning (leader's name); good morning to all.'
All adults present: 'Good morning children.'

INTRODUCTION

Our Assembly today is about the five senses.

The five senses are seeing, hearing, touching, tasting and smelling. We all learn by taking in information through one or more of our senses. As you no doubt know, some people are unable to see, some cannot hear and others are unable to taste, smell or feel. Which sights do you enjoy most? Close your eyes and use your 'third' eye inside your head to see a picture in your mind of something you really like to see. (Pause) Open your eyes again.

What are your favourite sounds?

Which smells do you enjoy most? Which do you enjoy least?

What are your favourite foods? What do you not like?
Which objects do you like to touch?

PRAYER

Let us talk to God.
Dear God, we thank you for the gift of our senses. Help us to appreciate the wonders of the world, especially those we can see or hear. We thank you for being able to smell and taste. We thank you for the sensitivity of our fingers and the ability to enjoy the sense of touch. Amen.

The Lord's Prayer (if desired)

Hymn
He gave me eyes so I could see (*Come and Praise* 18).
Think of a world without any flowers (*Come and Praise* 17).

Bible Reference
The Blind Man Healed (St Mark ch. 10 vv 46–52).
The Deaf Man Healed (St Mark ch.7 vv 32–37).

CONTENT

One day, five children were each asked to write down the things they enjoyed most – using the five senses. These are the lists they compiled.

David

The three things I like to see most are:

1. My favourite team scoring a goal.
2. My dad's face when he laughs.
3. Wildlife programmes on television.

Diane

The three things I like most to hear are:

1. My mum's voice.
2. Music — like singing.
3. Money rattling in my money box!

Judith

The three things I like best to smell are:

1. Perfume that my older sister uses.
2. Grass when the lawn is being mown.
3. Barbecued food.

Sarah

The three things I like best to taste are:

1. Spaghetti Bolognaise.
2. Salt spray on my lips when I'm sailing.
3. Chocolate fudge.

Henry

The three things I like most to touch are:

1. My dog when I stroke her.

2. Conkers.

3. A warm radiator on a cold day.

I wonder what you would have chosen?

Hymn
All things bright and beautiful (*Come and Praise* 3).
Thank you, Lord, for this new day (*Come and Praise* 32).

CLOSING PRAYER

We all join together to say:

May the Lord keep us all in his care. May he watch over those whom we love, and those who love us. Amen.

Closing music
Quiet, very short piece of music.
Any necessary announcements

Recessional music
Children leave at the close of the Assembly whilst appropriate music is played (by pianist, group, orchestra or recording).

For younger children
(For involvement before, during or after assembly.)

● Try to guess what objects there are in a 'Feely Bag' (using touch only).

● Say or write down things that you do not like to see, hear, taste, touch or smell.

● Make a collection of small objects that you like to touch because you like to feel or stroke them.

For older children
(For involvement before, during or after assembly.)

● Consider the possibility of a 'sixth sense' (intuition?). Tell about any experience you have had or heard about using a 'sixth sense'.

● How can we help people who are disabled because they lack one or more of the five senses?

● Try to obtain a piece of Braille and show how the sense of touch can be substituted for the sense of sight when a blind person reads.

Some further suggestions

● A blind person with his/her guide dog could be invited to the Assembly to give a brief talk about how the dog is trained and how it uses its senses to help its owner.

● A demonstration of sign language could be arranged to show how it is possible to talk to a hearing impaired person.

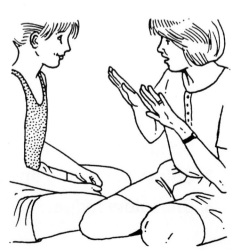

BURIED TREASURE

Opening Music
As the children enter for Assembly, suitable music is played by a pianist, a group of musicians, members of the school orchestra, or from a recording.

GREETING

Leader: 'Good morning children.'

Children: 'Good morning (Leader's name); Good morning everyone.'
All adults present: 'Good morning children.'

INTRODUCTION

Our Assembly today is called 'Buried Treasure'.

The buried treasure is not gold, silver, diamonds or precious stones but one day it may be like a rare gem!

Here are three questions which you do not need to answer, but I want you to think about. Later in this Assembly you will see how the three questions are connected.

1. Have you ever been to London?

2. Do you know what a time capsule is?

3. Can you think of anything that never changes with the passing of time?

PRAYER

Let us pray. Heavenly Father, may our words, actions and thoughts please you this and every day. We thank you for watching over us throughout the past night and for bringing us safely to the beginning of this day. Please accept our praises and our love.

Amen.

The Lord's Prayer (if desired).

Hymn
Come and praise the Lord our King (*Come and Praise* 21).
From the darkness came light (*Come and Praise* 29).

Bible Reference
'For God loved the world so much that he gave his only Son, so that everyone who believes in him may not die but have eternal life'. (Good News Bible, St John ch 3 v 16.)

CONTENT

Can those of you who have been to London tell us the names of some of the famous places and things you saw?

One of the oldest things in London is situated on the Thames' Embankment. It is called Cleopatra's Needle and this is its story.

Cleopatra's Needle is the name given to a sixty-eight foot tall column of pink granite weighing one hundred and eighty tons. It was given its nickname in 1878 by Londoners when it was set up on its present site. This column of stone, or obelisk, is one of a pair, and the other one stands in Central Park, in New York.

Both obelisks began life over three thousand years ago in Heliopolis, Egypt where they were shaped and later carved with hieroglyphics. In 10 BC they were taken to Alexandria to decorate a new palace. In 1819, the Viceroy of Egypt presented one of the obelisks to Britain. In 1877 a special tube-shaped raft was designed to ship the stone to England. This cigar shaped raft carrying the obelisk was towed to the Port of London. The voyage was difficult and dangerous. Six seamen lost their lives when trying to recover the raft after it broke free from its tow rope during a storm in the Bay of Biscay.
Eventually the great stone reached London and it was erected on its present site in 1878.

When it was set up it was decided to bury some objects under its plinth. It was suggested that the items chosen should be of interest to any persons finding them possibly many hundreds of years later. The following objects were placed in an airtight box (or time capsule) and buried under the Needle:

Some hairgrips and a safety pin.

A smoker's pipe.

Coins of the realm dated 1878.

A set of weights.

A London daily newspaper.

Some toys and books.

A railway time-table.

A baby's feeding bottle.

A set of photographs of some of the most beautiful women of the time!

Finally it was decided that as all the above objects would change with time, something should be included that would never ever change.

It was agreed that the truth of the text from St John's Gospel chapter 3 verse 16 would never change. The verse was written out in over two hundred languages known in 1878, and placed in the capsule. These are the words that were written out: 'God so loved the world that He gave His only begotten Son, that whosoever believeth on Him should not perish but have everlasting life.'

If ever you visit London and walk along the Thames' embankment, look for Cleopatra's Needle and remember the strange things that are buried under its plinth.

Hymn
At the name of Jesus (*Come and Praise* 58).
I danced in the morning (*Come and Praise* 22).

CLOSING PRAYER

Let us together say:

May the Lord keep us all in his care. May he watch over those whom we love and those who love us.

Amen.

Closing music
A very short, quiet, piano piece.
Any necessary announcements.

Recessional music
Children leave at the close of assembly whilst appropriate music is played (by pianist, group, orchestra or recording).

For younger children
(For involvement before, during or after assembly.)

- Make a scrapbook of pictures of 'Famous London Landmarks'.

- What ordinary things which you use every day might be of interest to someone who finds them in a thousand years' time?

- Visit your local museum and look at ordinary objects which were used, say, a hundred years ago.

For older children
(For involvement before, during or after assembly.)

- Make a list of the names of objects you would put in a time capsule. Why do you think they would be of interest to someone who may find them many years later?

- Make a time capsule. Put in it some interesting everyday objects.

- Make up a dance drama using 'futuristic' music. Dress in 'futuristic' fashion or costume, then, interpreting the music, imagine you find the time capsule in a thousand years time. Open the chest and show the objects you find.

Further suggestion
If your school (or associated building) is being re-built or extended, prepare a time capsule. Consider carefully what to put in it. (Perhaps include a home-made video with your own commentary). Arrange a time capsule burying ceremony. (Perhaps invite the local press or others to photograph the event.)

COLOUR

Opening music
Music is played by a pianist, group, school orchestra or from a recording as the children enter for assembly.

GREETING

Leader: 'Good morning children.'

Children: 'Good morning (leader's name); good morning to all.'
All adults present: 'Good morning children.'

INTRODUCTION

Have you ever thought how dull this world would be without colour? Do you have a favourite colour? If you have a favourite colour, why did you choose it? (Pause — and ask a few children to tell their favourite colours, and why they chose them.)

Did you know that the most restful colour for our eyes is said to be green. Perhaps that is why nature has green as its most used colour! God must have been a wonderful and sensible artist. Can you imagine what it would be like if all the grass in the world was red!

Are there any colours you dislike? Why?

As you will have gathered, our assembly today is about colour.

PRAYER

Let us close our eyes, bow our heads and put our hands together as we say our prayer:

For the beauty of colour we thank you, God. For the blue of the sky and the gold of sunlight; the greens and browns of trees; the differing pinks and mauves of flowers; the white of snow and clouds and for all the colours of the rainbow we give you our joyful thanks.

Amen.

The Lord's Prayer (if desired).

Hymn
Who put the colours in the rainbow? (*Come and Praise 12*).
Daisies are our silver.

Bible reference
Colours in the tent Church (Select verses from Exodus, chapters 25 and 26).

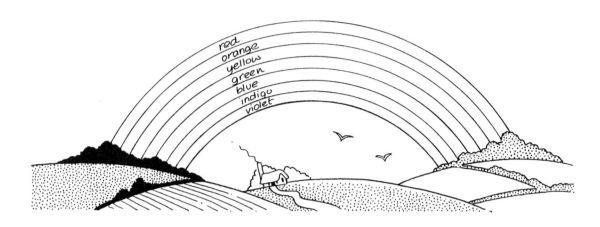

red
orange
yellow
green
blue
indigo
violet

CONTENT

Can you say with me the colours of the rainbow?

Red, orange, yellow, green, blue, indigo and violet. One way of remembering them in order is to say R O Y G B I V, or 'Richard of York gained battles in vain'.

Did you know that white light is a mixture of all the colours of the rainbow, or spectrum? When you look at anything that has a colour, you can see the colour because the object you are looking at has absorbed all the colours from white light and is reflecting just the colour you see.

Colourful things seem to make people happy. I wonder why so many people have black umbrellas? When it is raining and the weather is miserable perhaps we should try to cheer ourselves up by using brightly coloured umbrellas!

I wonder how you would try to describe colour to a person who has been blind since birth? Or what a person, blind since birth, imagines colour to be like? Listen to this poem called 'Colour':

I asked the little boy who cannot see,
'And what is colour like?'
— 'Why, green,' said he,
'Is like the rustle when the wind blows through
The forest; running water, that is blue;
And red is like a trumpet sound; and pink
Is like the smell of roses; and I think
That purple must be like a thunderstorm;
And yellow is like something soft and warm;
And white is a pleasant stillness when you lie
And dream.'

J.M. MacDougall Ferguson

Now, close your eyes and I will read the poem again, slowly. Imagine you are the blind boy while I read.

(Read the poem again slowly).

Open your eyes. You are able to see and enjoy all the lovely colours in this beautiful world.

Hymn
Colours of day dawn into the mind (*Come and Praise* 55).
All things bright and beautiful (*Come and Praise* 3).

CLOSING PRAYER

We join together to say: May the Lord keep us all in his care. May he watch over those whom we love, and those who love us.

Amen.

Closing music
A very short, quiet piece is played.

Any necessary announcements

Recessional music
Music, by the pianist, group, orchestra or recording is played as the children leave.

For younger children
(For involvement before, during or after assembly.)

- Draw and name colours using crayons or paint ('colours I like' and/or 'colours I do not like').

- Collect objects of the same colour (with teacher's help, set up a colour corner).

- Experiment by mixing together different coloured paints. What happens?

- Make a block graph showing the favourite colours of your class members.

For older children
(For involvement before, during or after assembly.)

- Make a colour wheel using the spectrum colours (try spinning it for 'white light').

- Use a prism and source of light to project a spectrum.

- Find out and write or tell about 'animal camouflage'.

- Try to obtain some colour-blind test cards. How are they used?

- How are colours used as warning signals by humans or in the natural world?

- Make a colour spiral, using one colour of paint and introducing others gradually.

- Design Joseph's coat of many colours.

CHILDREN WELCOME!

Opening music
As the children enter, suitable music is played by a pianist, group, school orchestra, or recording.

GREETING

Leader: 'Good morning children.'

Children: 'Good morning (leader's name); good morning to all.'
All adults present: 'Good morning children.'

INTRODUCTION

Do you like being the age you are, or would you prefer to be a grown up? Do you find that older people treat you politely, listen to what you have to say, and are generally kind to you? In Victorian times it was said that children should be seen and not heard! How do you treat grown-ups? Do you show them respect, listen to their advice and behave politely towards them?

Listen carefully: Someone once said that all children should remember that one day they may be old, and that all old people should remember that they were once young! Our assembly today is about children and being kind to them.

Hymn
There are hundreds of sparrows, thousands, millions (*Come and Praise* 15).
Think of a world without any flowers (*Come and Praise* 17).

PRAYER

Lord Jesus we know that you loved children and were friendly towards them. We know that you watched them play and when mothers brought their children to see you, you took the children up in your arms, sat them on your knee and blessed them. Please bless us and watch over us in our work and play.

Amen.

The Lord's Prayer (if desired).

Bible reference
Jesus Blesses Little Children, St Mark ch 10 vv 13–16.

CONTENT

The noise of happy children's voices when playing can be a joyful sound, but I am not sure that I would like to live next door to a school playground!

This story is about a giant and his huge garden.

The children loved to play in the giant's garden. It was beautiful, especially in the spring time when the flowers and the cherry trees blossomed and the birds sang.

One day the giant came out and shouted very loudly at the children. With an angry voice he called out, 'What are you doing here? This is my garden and you are not allowed to play in it. Go away and keep out!'

Then the giant built a high wall all around his garden so that the children could not enter. He put up large notices which said 'Private Property. Keep Out'.

When the spring came, all the countryside around the garden looked fresh with dancing flowers and bursting buds. The birds whistled and new-born lambs skipped in the fields; but not in the giant's garden where it was still winter with frost and snow covering everything and cruel winds blowing.

'I wonder why the spring is so late coming to my garden?' said the giant to himself. 'I hope the weather improves quickly for summer will soon be here'. Indeed summer did arrive soon, to every other garden except the giant's garden where it remained like winter. Autumn came too and there were many ripe apples in the other gardens, but not in his.

The giant was sad and worried. Then, one day, he heard a beautiful sound. It was a linnet singing in one of his trees. He looked out and had a shock. All the children who used to play in his garden had found their way in through a small hole in his high wall. They had crept in stealthily and now there was a child sitting in every one of his trees. The sun was shining, the flowers were blooming, the grass was clear of white frost and snow and was green again and the trees had burst into leaf and blossom.

'What a glorious sight,' thought the giant, but as he looked, he noticed that one corner of his garden was still like winter. Then he saw that a small boy was standing in that corner. The boy was so small he could not climb the trees. The tree near him was drooping its branches and was covered in frost.

'How selfish I have been', said the giant as he smiled at last. 'Now I know why spring, summer and autumn would not come to my garden. I will lift that little boy into the branches of the tree and I will knock down the high wall and invite all the children to come and play in my garden whenever they wish.'

The giant went quietly into the garden but the children saw him and ran away as fast as they could because they were afraid of him. When the children left, the garden immediately turned wintry again. Only the little boy remained. He was crying because he could not climb the trees and as his eyes were full of tears he did not see the giant coming. The giant crept up behind the little boy and lifted him very gently into the tree. At once the tree broke into blossom and the birds flew to sing in its branches. The boy smiled and knew that the giant was friendly.

The other children saw what had happened and they came running back. The giant knocked down the wall, and, as the children re-entered the garden, the spring came with them. For ever afterwards spring, summer, autumn and winter came in turns to the giant's garden and he was pleased because the children played there all the time.

(Re-told from Oscar Wilde.)

Hymn
When God made the garden of creation (*Come and Praise* 16).
In our dear Lord's garden.

CLOSING PRAYER

We say together:

May the Lord keep us all in his care. May he watch over those whom we love, and those who love us.

Amen.

Closing music
Quiet, very short piece of music.

Any necessary announcements

Recessional music
Children leave at the close of assembly whilst appropriate music is played by pianist, group, orchestra or from a recording.

For younger children
(For involvement before, during or after assembly.)

- Paint and show a picture of the giant's garden.

- Listen to, or tell stories about giants.

For older children
(For involvement before, during or after assembly.)

- Find, read and possibly tell stories about giants (e.g. David and Goliath; Giant Despair in *Pilgrim's Progress*; the giant in *The B.F.G.* by Roald Dahl).

- Act out the story of *The Giant's Garden.*

DONKEYS

GREETING

Leader: 'Good morning children.'

Children: 'Good morning (leader's name); good morning to all.'
All adults present: 'Good morning children.'

INTRODUCTION

Do you like donkeys? Have you ever ridden on a donkey? Have you ever heard a donkey bray? I think donkeys have kind but rather sad looking faces. They have lovely long soft ears. It is said that every donkey has the mark of a cross on its back with a dark line of fur running down its back and a shorter line of dark fur crossing between its withers (shoulders). When you next see a donkey, look for the cross on its back. Legend has it that the cross has been on  a donkey's back ever since Jesus rode on a donkey when he entered Jerusalem in triumph on the first Palm Sunday.

PRAYER

Let us talk to God.

Lord Jesus, we remember that when you rode into Jerusalem on the first Palm Sunday, children waved and welcomed you with loud shouts of joy. Teach us to praise and welcome you always, whether our days are filled with happiness or sadness.

Amen.

The Lord's Prayer (if desired).

Hymn
Ride on! Ride on in majesty!
Trotting, trotting through Jerusalem (*Come and Praise* 128).

Bible Reference
The Triumphant Entry Into Jerusalem, (St Matthew ch 21 vv 1–11).

CONTENT

People who are sometimes stubborn or silly are jokingly, and rather cruelly, called 'Donkeys'. Here is a story called 'The Miller, the Son and the Donkey' — or should it be three donkeys! The lesson we should learn from the story is, 'Think for yourself'.

A man and his son set out one day to go to market to buy some provisions. They took their donkey to carry the goods home.

As they walked they met a man who said, 'Why does not one of you ride on the donkey as it is a long way to market?'

The father and son considered this remark and decided that it would be sensible for the father to ride.

They had not travelled far when they heard a passer-by exclaim, 'Look at that lazy father who rides on a donkey whilst his poor son has to walk!'

The father was upset when he heard this remark and immediately jumped down from the donkey's back and put his son to ride in his place.

They had not travelled much further when they met a third stranger who cried, 'How foolish you are! Why walk when you may ride? Why do you not both ride on the donkey?'

The father and son thought about this last suggestion and, as it was not now far to market, they decided to take the advice and both clambered on the donkey's back.

They were soon passed by a woman who shouted out indignantly, 'Look at these two lazy, cruel, good-for-nothings! They do not deserve to own such a willing and lovely beast. Fancy both sitting on the poor donkey's back when they are both perfectly fit to walk! It is they who should be carrying the donkey, not the donkey carrying them!'

On hearing this the father and son slid down from the donkey's back. They both felt very guilty and ashamed. With great difficulty they lifted up the donkey and tried to carry it to market!

They had not gone very far when they came to a narrow bridge over a stream. As they tried to carry the donkey across, they slipped and all three fell into the water. Luckily it was not deep and they soon managed to clamber out. The father and son were wet and looked rather foolish. Many villagers stood watching and laughing. They cried, 'Look at the three wet donkeys coming to market!'

Perhaps the father and son learned a lesson — to think for themselves in future!

(Re-told from A.G. Patston.)

Hymn
All glory, laud and honour.
The journey of life (*Come and Praise* 45).

CLOSING PRAYER

We all join together to say:

May the Lord keep us all in his care. May he watch over those whom we love, and those who love us.

Amen.

Closing music
At the end of the closing prayer, the pianist plays a few bars of quiet music, unannounced, whilst all remain still and quiet.
Any necessary announcements.

Recessional music
Children leave the assembly whilst appropriate music is played by a pianist, group or school orchestra, or from a recording.

For younger children
(For involvement before, during or after assembly.)
- Act out or mime the story.
- Find and play, if possible, the card game called 'Donkey'.
- Make a class picture, frieze or mural depicting Palm Sunday.
- Play the game of pinning the tail on the donkey!

For older children
(For involvement before, during or after assembly.)
- Find and read the well known poem 'The Donkey' by G. K. Chesterton.
- Dramatise the story of the father, son and their donkey.
- Discuss: 'When should you act on advice given by others?'

Additional material
Poem
Tired Donkey
Dozy donkey with drooping head,
Nibble through the grassy bed.
Drowsily, browsily, graze your way;
Idly stray throughout the day

Exhausting races on the sands;
Adoring children's patting hands
Forget! Flop-eared, cross blessed,
Drool, and enjoy a well-earned rest!
Terry Gilbert

20

TWICE MINE

Opening music
As the children enter, suitable music is played by soloist (piano?), group (recorders?), orchestra or from pre-recorded tape/record/CD.

GREETING

Leader: 'Good morning children.'

Children: 'Good morning (leader's name). 'Good morning to all.'
All adults present: 'Good morning children.'

INTRODUCTION

Do you like making things? Do you ever make things from construction kits or junk material?

Do you ever have help from parents or grown-ups?

Put your hands up if your parents are good at D I Y. (Hands down.)

Put your hands up if your parents are not good at D I Y! (Hands down.)

Some parents and children are very skilful at using their fingers and hands to make all sorts of lovely things or to do all kinds of jobs. Today's story is about a boy and his model boat. We are thinking about Easter and our hymns and prayer remind us of the Easter story.

PRAYER

Let us pray. Dear God, we think about the first Easter and we remember the great sacrifice that Jesus made when he gave his life that we might live. Fill our hearts with wonder and gladness and help us to understand the meaning of the Easter Story.

Amen.

The Lord's Prayer (if desired).

Hymn
There is a green hill far away.
From the darkness came light (*Come and Praise* 29).

Bible Reference
The First Easter Story — read extracts from St Mark ch. 15 vv 16–31 or St Mark ch.15 vv 33-39.

CONTENT

John's Model Boat

John was your age and he loved to make things. Sometimes he made models from construction kits but on other occasions he used his imagination and used odds and ends to create things like miniature toys.

One day, with his father's help, John made a model sailing boat. It was definitely the best thing he had ever made.

With his parents, John took his boat to the local park where there was a pond. He wanted to see if would sail as well as it looked.

As the light breeze filled its tiny sails, the boat sailed easily and smoothly across the small lake. It really moved beautifully across the water.

Next, John decided that he would like to sail his boat on the sea. He attached one end of a long length of twine to his model and wound the other end round a short stick. Unfortunately, John forgot to tie the end of the twine to the stick.

The little boat drifted out from the sandy beach. It skipped lightly over the waves and seemed to dance its way out to sea. Further and further it sailed, trailing the thread. Then, can you guess what happened?

The end of the twine which was not tied to the stick dropped off and the little model boat disappeared from sight as it continued its lonely voyage out to sea. David watched tearfully because he thought that his boat was lost for ever. Even his father's offer to help make a new boat did not console him.

One day, several weeks later, John was amazed to see his boat in the window of the local model shop. He could hardly believe his eyes. He stared at the model and then noticed a price tag attached to its mast.

John rushed into the shop and explained to the shopkeeper how he had designed, built, sailed and then lost his boat which was now in the shop window. John then asked the shopkeeper if he could have his boat back!

The shopkeeper, who was a kindly man, listened sympathetically to John's story but then explained that he had bought the boat from a local fisherman who had found it entangled in his net. The shopkeeper said that he would keep the boat for John until he was able to pay the same amount that he had given the fisherman.

John raced home. He turned out his money box and counted out enough money to pay for his boat. He then hurried back to the shop and the shopkeeper handed him back his model in exchange for the payment.

John was overjoyed. He clasped the boat tightly. As he left the shop the shopkeeper overheard John muttering to himself. He heard him say, 'You're mine twice. I made you and I bought you at a price!'

Hymn
I danced in the morning (*Come and Praise* 22).
Now the green blade rises (*Come and Praise* 131).

CLOSING PRAYER

We say together:

May the Lord keep us all in his care. May he watch over those whom we love and those who love us.

Amen.

Closing music
A very short piece of music is played whilst all present quietly meditate for a few moments.
Any necessary announcements.

Recessional music
As the children leave, suitable music is played by soloist, group, orchestra or from a recording.

For younger children
(For involvement before, during or after assembly.)
- Make a model using junk material. (It does not have to be a sailing boat.) Show how it works.
- Paint a picture of a model boat

For older children
(For involvement before, during or after assembly.)
- Construct a working model using a construction kit (e.g. Technic Lego). You may follow a suggested plan.
- Make a model sailing boat that does not capsize!

Further suggestions
- Arrange an exhibition of models.
- Show individual- or group-made models in Assembly.
- Start a Lego (or similar) model club.

EASTER EGGS AND BIRDS

Opening music
As children enter and take their places, music is played by the pianist, group, school orchestra or from a recording.

GREETING

Leader: 'Good morning children.'

Children: 'Good morning (leader's name); good morning everyone.'
All adults present: 'Good morning children.'

INTRODUCTION

Springtime and Easter is the time when many birds are nest building. It is also the time we associate with eggs, chocolate and other kinds – and newly hatched chicks. There is a lovely German legend about some poor mothers who could not afford to buy Easter sweets for their children so they hid hen's eggs, all painted different colours, in the fields and under the bushes near their homes. The children were very thrilled and excited to find red, blue, pink and yellow eggs hidden in the grass. They were mystified and could not think what kind of bird  could have laid them. Then they saw a hare run out from the hedgerow and decided that the hare had laid the eggs. 'Three cheers for the Easter Hare which laid the coloured eggs!' they shouted.

I am not sure that you will find any hare's eggs this Easter, but I hope you may find other eggs that you like!

In our assembly today we are going to hear about three different kinds of birds, each of which has an Easter link – the cockerel, the pelican and the phoenix.

Hymn
I danced in the morning (*Come and Praise* 22).
Come and praise the Lord our King, Hallelujah (*Come and Praise* 21).

PRAYER

We thank you, Heavenly Father, that springtime reminds us of the first Easter when you died but then rose again to be with us always, and to bring us new life every day. Help us to feel that you are near to us today and always.

Amen.

The Lord's Prayer (if desired).

Bible Reference
Peter's Denial: St. Matthew ch 26 vv 31–35; 69–75.

CONTENT

The Cockerel

If you look on the top of a church spire you may see a weather vane. It is really a wind vane and usually it has the figure of a gold-coloured cockerel which always points towards the direction of the wind. The cockerel was chosen by early church builders for two reasons. First, they wished to remind the people of the need to be on the look-out for evil and always to be wide awake, just like the cockerel who is the first  to greet the new day at dawn with his 'Cock-a-doodle-doo-o-o-o', and, second, to remind people of the story about Peter who denied knowing Jesus three times before a cock crowed — just as Jesus had predicted.

The Pelican

This is a rather gruesome story but it ends happily.

Did you know that there is a stone carved figure of a pelican on the wall of Truro Cathedral? Why a pelican, which is a rather strange looking bird?

Many, many years ago people said that three days after young pelicans had hatched from their eggs, the mother pelican would kill them. Then, she would peck at her own breast until she bled. When the drops of blood from her breast fell on her dead chicks they would immediately come to life again.

The story reminded people of the death of Jesus; how he died by shedding his blood; how he rose again after three days and was seen alive on the first Easter Day.

The Phoenix

To remind themselves of Jesus' crucifixion, death and resurrection, people used to tell the story of the phoenix, a bird that never actually existed.

It was said that there was only ever one phoenix in the world at one time. This bird was supposed to build a nest every five hundred years. When the phoenix sat on its nest, a fire would spring up and burn the nest and bird. Then, a new phoenix would arise from the ashes and live for five hundred years, and start the life cycle all over again.

I wonder if there are any more stories about eggs or birds at Easter?

Hymn
From the darkness came light (*Come and Praise* 29).
Jesus, good above all other (*Come and Praise* 23).

CLOSING PRAYER

Let us say together:

May the Lord keep us all in his care. May he watch over those whom we love, and those who love us.

Amen.

Closing music
Pianist plays a few bars of quiet music whist all present bow heads in silent contemplation.
Any necessary announcements.

Recessional music
Music is played by a pianist, group, school orchestra or from a recording as children and adults leave.

For younger children
(For involvement before, during or after assembly.)

- Make paper or card Easter egg baskets and put in small Easter eggs.
- Hatch some eggs in an incubator in the classroom.
- Find out about (and possibly engage in) other Easter customs (e.g. make: hot cross buns; Easter bonnets or Easter fluffy chicks).
- Paint, hide and seek some 'Hare's Eggs'!

For older children
(For involvement before, during or after assembly.)

- Arrange a decorated Easter egg competition (using hard boiled eggs).
- Dismantle a used bird's nest and separate out all the materials used in its construction.
- Find out and write about different kinds of eggs of various animals. How are the eggs and newly hatched creatures protected?
- Paint a large colourful picture of a phoenix rising out of its burning nest.

FRIGHTENING FEATHERS

Opening music
Music is played by the pianist, group, school orchestra or from a recording as the children assemble. (An extract from Dvorak's *9th Symphony* 'From the New World' would be appropriate.)

GREETING

Leader: 'Good morning children.'

Children: 'Good morning (leader's name); good morning to all.'
All adults present: 'Good morning children.'

INTRODUCTION

Western films are usually about cowboys and Indians. The cowboys always seem to be the 'goodies' and the Indians are usually the 'baddies'.

When you grow older you may come to learn more about the Indians and their customs; their great love for the earth and especially their own lands. Red Indians are now usually called Native Americans, because they lived in America long before white and black people arrived from other countries and began to live there too.

Native Americans worship different gods but the Great Spirit is their chief God, who, they believe, guides them and has to be obeyed.

Hymn
Peace, perfect peace, is the gift of Christ our Lord (*Come and Praise* 53).
The King of love my shepherd is (*Come and Praise* 54).

PRAYER

Dear Lord, we thank you for watching over us at all times and in all places. Help us to remember that you are always near. We give you our thanks for all your loving care.

Amen.

The Lord's Prayer (if desired).

Bible Reference
'God will cover you with his feathers and you will be safe under the wings of his care. You need not fear the arrow that flies by day nor the dangers of the night'. Psalm 91 vv 4–5 (adapted).

CONTENT

When the Pilgrim Fathers first landed in America, food was scarce. The Pilgrims learned from the Native Americans how to grow crops. Unfortunately trouble broke out between some of the early settlers and the Native Americans whose land was being occupied. Some of the Native Americans were driven from their lands and fierce battles were fought.

Many white settlers fled when the Native Americans began burning their log cabins but one group of settlers, Quakers, who did not believe in fighting or violence, decided to stay. They worshipped regularly in their log-built Meeting House.

One Sunday, as usual, the Quaker children sat in the wooden Meeting House waiting for a visiting minister to arrive. Their parents sat quietly behind them and were pleased when the old man who was visiting them arrived. He had travelled twenty miles through the forest and came from another Quaker settlement.

He told the children of God's love for them. He said that the Lord would watch over them at all times and he would 'cover them with his feathers'. The children thought of their own hens and how they protected their chicks by using their wings to shelter them.

The children were thinking about feathers when, suddenly, they noticed a feather which flicked across the open square window behind the minister's head. They saw another feather then another and another then, finally, the war-painted face and flashing teeth of a Native American brave glaring at them from the window.

The children were terrified and when they turned round they saw a Native American chief in full war dress, with twelve braves standing at the open door of their Meeting House. The fierce-looking warriors fitted arrows to their bows and took aim at the old Quaker, but he did not flinch.

The braves waited for their chief to give the order to shoot and kill the Quaker. Then a strange thing happened. The Native American chief raised his hand to stop his braves from shooting their arrows. Very slowly they lowered their bows at his command. The chief said, 'Indians come to white man's house to kill white man. White man worship Great Spirit. Great Spirit in Indian say 'No kill. No kill.'

Then the chief took from his head-dress a white feather which he offered to the old Quaker. The Quaker stepped forward and took the white feather, which was a sign of friendship. The chief and his braves turned and left as quickly and as silently as they had come, and never again were the Quakers threatened by the Native Americans.

(Based on 'Fierce Feathers', a story in L. Violet Hodgkin's A *Book of Quaker Saints*.)

Hymn
Spirit of God, as strong as the wind (*Come and Praise* 63).
The Lord's my shepherd, I'll not want (*Come and Praise* 56).

CLOSING PRAYER

We say together:

May the Lord keep us all in his care. May he watch over those whom we love, and those who love us.

Amen.

Closing music
A few bars of quiet music are played by the pianist whilst all present listen in silence.
Any necessary announcements.

Recessional music
The pianist, group or school orchestra play whilst all leave. Alternatively a recording is played.
(Music suitable — excerpts from Dvorak's *9th Symphony* 'From the New World'.)

For younger children
(For involvement before, during or after assembly.)

- Make and display a collection of feathers.

- Paint a picture of a Native American brave's war-painted face.

- Find out about Native Americans and their customs.

For older children
(For involvement before, during or after assembly.)

- Find and read extracts from H. W. Longfellow's *Hiawatha*.

- Act out parts of *Hiawatha* or devise a dance drama of the story using excerpts from Dvorak's 9th Symphony (which was partly inspired by Longfellow's *Hiawatha*).

- If possible, visit the American Museum at Claverton (near Bath).

- Find out about the Pilgrim Fathers.

Additional material
(An early indication of the Native Americans' love for their land and environment.)

God's Land

Every part of this earth is sacred. Every single pine needle, every shore, every mist in the dark woods, every clearing, every humming insect is holy in the memory and experience of our race. You are part of the earth and the earth is part of you.

You did not weave the web of life; you are merely a strand in it. Whatever you do to the web, you do to yourself. You may think you own the land. You do not. It is God's. The earth is precious to Him and to harm the earth is to heap contempt on its Creator.

Love the land as those who have gone before you have loved it. Care for it as they have cared for it. Hold in your mind the memory of the land as it is when you take it.

And with all your strength, with all your mind, with all your heart, preserve it for your children and love it ... as God loves us all.

Chief Seattle 1854

BREAD

Preparation
Some of the following items, not necessarily on view at the outset, could be shown during the assembly:

> A bread roll or loaf, made by the leader; not necessarily of good quality!
>
> The various ingredients needed to make bread (flour, water, salt, milk, yeast etc.)
>
> Five small loaves and two small fishes.

Opening music
Music by a pianist, group, orchestra or from a recording is played as the children assemble.

GREETING

Leader: 'Good morning children.'

Children: 'Good morning (leader's name); good morning everybody.'
All adults present: 'Good morning children.'

INTRODUCTION

How many of you have tried to make bread? I have made some bread and here is the loaf/roll that I made. Would anyone like to try a piece?

(Break the bread (which may be difficult!) and share out.)

Put up your hands and tell me what ingredients you need to make bread.

(As the various items are called out, show them).

Now tell me how the ingredients should be used to make the bread.

(It may be possible actually to mix the ingredients together, if the right quantities have been prepared.)

What does it mean to knead (not need!) bread? Bread needs to be kneaded! Do you know what it means to 'prove' bread?

(To cause or allow the dough to rise).

Why is yeast so important when making bread?

Our assembly today is all about bread.

Let us sing together our first hymn.

Hymn
The earth is yours, O God (*Come and Praise* 6).
Now the harvest is all gathered (*Come and Praise* 139).

PRAYER

Jesus said, 'I am the bread of life'. Lord, we often, in our prayers, say 'Give us this day our daily bread'. Dear Father we thank you for your gift of food, and especially bread. Help us never to waste food and always to be ready to share what we have with those in need.

Amen.

The Lord's Prayer (said or sung (*Come and Praise* 51) if desired).

Bible reference
Manna from Heaven (Exodus ch 16 vv 2–4).
Jesus the Bread of Life (St John ch 6 vv 35 and 48).

CONTENT

When Jesus welcomed the disciples at The Last Supper, he blessed and broke the bread. He did the same when he appeared to the disciples on the shores of the Sea of Galilee and in Emmaus after his resurrection.

Listen to this lovely verse, about bread:

Be gentle when you touch bread.

Let it not lie uncared for, unwanted.

So often bread is taken for granted.

There is such beauty in bread.

Beauty of sun and soil,

Beauty of patient toil.

Wind and rain have caressed it,

Christ often blessed it,

Be gentle when you touch bread.

(From *Flowing Streams*, NCEC.)

One of the best known miracle stories in the Bible is that of the feeding of five thousand people with only five loaves and two fishes. Here is the story of the loaves and fishes.

One day when Jesus and his disciples landed from the boat in which they had been resting, they were met by a vast crowd of people who had come from nearby towns and villages to see and hear Jesus.

Jesus preached to them and, as it grew late, the disciples suggested that the great multitude should return to their homes and seek food on their way.

Jesus told his disciples to feed the people before they left but the disciples explained that they had no food and in any case there were far too many to feed.

Then the disciple Andrew said that a small boy in the crowd had offered his picnic lunch of five barley loaves and two fish.

Jesus told the people to sit down on the grass. He took the bread, blessed and broke it. He gave the divided loaves and fishes to the disciples to distribute to the people. Everyone had enough to eat and when they had finished, twelve baskets were filled with the scraps.

The number of people fed was five thousand.

(Re-told from St. Luke's Gospel.)

Hymn
When God made the garden of creation (*Come and Praise* 16).
Lord of the harvest, Lord of the field (*Come and Praise* 133).

CLOSING PRAYER

We join together to say:

May the Lord keep us all in his care; may he watch over those whom we love, and those who love us.

Amen.

Closing music
A few bars of quiet music are played by the pianist whilst all present reflect and meditate in silence.
Any necessary announcements.

Recessional music
Appropriate music is played by the pianist, group, school orchestra or by recording as the children leave.

For younger children
(For involvement before, during or after assembly.)

- Children, in groups or individually, make bread — under supervision.

- Find out and write down the ingredients needed to make bread.

- Draw a picture of five barley rolls and two small fishes.

For older children
(For involvement before, during or after assembly.)

- Find out and list the names of different kinds of bread and write down the differences between them.

- Write out the recipes for making bread and chapattis, collect the ingredients and make both (under supervision).

- Visit a working flour mill.

- Find out about the nutritional and dietetic values of different kinds of bread.

ICHTHUS — The sign of the fish

Preparation

It is suggested that either a blackboard or large flip chart be set up at the front with the letters I C H T H U S written boldly in capitals across the top. Room on the board or chart should be left below the letters for a simple fish shape to be drawn during the assembly.

Opening music

Music should be played by a pianist, group, school orchestra or from a recording as the children enter.

GREETING

Leader: 'Good morning children.'

Children: 'Good morning (leader's name); good morning to all.'
All adults present: 'Good morning children.'

INTRODUCTION

I wonder how many of you collect things? What, if anything, do you collect? (Invite a few children to tell of their collections.) A boy living in Bristol, about your age, used to collect badges. He had hundreds of them. Some of them were mounted on card and others were sewn on to a large blanket. He had metal ones, plastic ones and some made of cloth. Each of his badges had a design, picture or message. Some of his badges signified membership of some organisation. If you saw someone wearing a small lapel badge in the shape of a fish, would you know why they were wearing it?

It is a badge sometimes worn by Christians.

Why a fish?

In this assembly you will hear the reason.

PRAYER

Lord Jesus, we will be still and quiet while we think about you. We remember that you were born in a stable in Bethlehem; that you walked in the fields, villages and towns of Galilee; that you preached to the people and healed the sick. We remember that you died on the cross and that you rose again on Easter Day. We remember that you promised to be with us always. Please be near us this morning as we praise you for your love and goodness to us.

Amen.

The Lord's Prayer (if desired).

Hymn
Come and praise the Lord our king (*Come and Praise* 21).
When Jesus walked in Galilee (*Come and Praise* 25).

Bible reference
'Tell that the Father sent His Son to be the Saviour of the world' (from 1 John ch 4 v 14).
'For God did not send His Son into the world to be its judge, but to be its Saviour' (St John ch 3 v 17).

CONTENT

The early Christians often met in secret because they were not allowed to worship publicly. They were often afraid because they were frequently hunted down and thrown into prison by those in authority.

The rulers tried to stop the Christians meeting together and they did everything possible to wipe out the memory of Jesus by persecuting his followers.

When the Christians did meet secretly in each other's houses they were careful not to admit strangers who might be enemies.

They decided that they would have a sign, like a pass-word and tried to choose one that they could all use.

The early Christians recognised that Jesus was the Son of God. The Greek words which said Jesus Christ, of God, Son and Saviour began with the letters I C H T H U S.

(Point to the letters on the board or chart.)

The Greek word 'ichthus' means 'fish'. So the early Christians decided that the fish would be their badge or emblem.

When they met each other they made the sign of the fish by 'drawing' its simple shape in the air, or by 'tracing' its shape on the palm of their friend's hand. This is the simple shape they drew in the air:

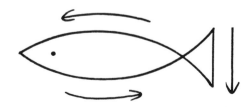

(The leader should 'draw' the simple shape in the air; then draw it on the board or chart. The eye of the fish is indicated by poking the forefinger forward after 'drawing' the simple outline shape of the fish. Let the children 'draw' the fish shape in the air using their forefingers and/or trace the shape in their palms.)

36

Hymn
There's a child in the streets (*Come and Praise* 27).
God is love; His the care (*Come and Praise* 36).

CLOSING PRAYER

We say together:

May the Lord keep us all in his care; may he watch over those whom we love, and those who love us.

Amen.

Closing music
The pianist plays a few bars of music whilst all sit in contemplative silence.
Any necessary announcements.

Recessional music
Children leave at the close of assembly whilst appropriate music is played by a pianist, group, school orchestra or from a recording.

For younger children
(For involvement before, during or after assembly.)

● The children could draw and cut out simple fish shapes which could then be painted or coloured.

● Make a fish mobile.

● Make badges using different designs to indicate different groups or organisations.

● Set up a 'Badge Corner' for a collection of badges brought in by the children.

For older children
(For involvement before, during or after assembly.)

● Find words which begin with 'ichth'. They usually have something to do with fish (e.g. Ichthyosaurus — prehistoric fish type reptile). Draw, name and show them.

● Design and make a badge with a safety-pin attachment, for some organisation of your choice.

● Make your own collection of badges, then mount and display them.

Links with other faiths
Find out, draw and display some of the signs and symbols of different religions.
Here are some: the Cross of Christianity, the eight-spoke wheel of Buddhism, the star and crescent moon of Islam, the star of David for Judaism, the om of Hinduism.

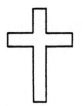    

JOHNNY'S MISSING

Opening music
As the children assemble, music is played by a pianist, group, school orchestra or from a recording.

GREETING

Leader: 'Good morning children.'

Children: 'Good morning (leader's name); good morning everybody.'
All adults present: 'Good morning children.'

INTRODUCTION

I expect most of you have a friend. Perhaps some of you have two or more special friends. Nod your head if you have got a 'Best Friend' or many friends. Point to your best friend. Point to all your friends!

Now, having settled down, have you ever thought what it must be like not to have friends? Perhaps there are children in your class or in this school who feel lonely even though they are surrounded by so many children of their own age. Teachers sometimes get worried if they often see the same boy or girl at playtime in the playground standing alone with no friend to play with or talk to. If you ever see someone like that, invite them to share in your game. I am sure you would like to help, if possible, to make a lonely boy or girl feel wanted. Our assembly today has a story to think about.

Hymn
Heavenly Father, may thy blessing (*Come and Praise* 62).
When I needed a neighbour, were you there, were you there? (*Come and Praise* 65).

PRAYER

Lord Jesus, you know how lovely friendships can be. Please bless our friends. Help us not to be jealous in our friendships and to share our friends with others. Teach us not to take offence easily or to be easily hurt. Help each one of us to be a loyal, generous and reliable friend. We know that you had special friends and that you gave your life for them and us. Please teach us how to grow more like you.

Amen.

The Lord's Prayer (if desired).

Bible reference
Friends, St John ch 15 vv 13–14.
Jesus chooses his special friends, St. Luke ch 6 vv 13–16.

CONTENT

The class was on an educational visit. It was evening now and they were ready to go home on the coach. The teacher counted the children and discovered that one boy was missing!

'Where's Johnny?' the teacher asked.

'Who?' they asked. 'Oh, Johnny. No idea. Somewhere or other. He'll turn up.'

They climbed aboard the bus.

'Where did you last see him?' asked the teacher.

No-one could remember seeing him; in fact one boy said, 'Did he come with us today?' 'He's always so quiet and he doesn't seem to have a proper friend,' said one of the girls. By now it was cold and the teacher and driver began to walk back to the woods where the class had been playing tracking earlier.

'Suppose something's happened to Johnny', said one of the boys.

All the children began making up frightening stories.

'Perhaps a wild boar has eaten him!' suggested one.

'Perhaps he got lost in the woods, broke his ankle or fell over the quarry edge', said another. They all laughed.

But now they were worried. Some of them got out and ran over to the edge of the wood and called out Johnny's name.

Inside the wood it looked very dark and they could not see their teacher or driver. They felt cold and frightened and returned to the coach.

Then the two men came back with Johnny. Nothing had happened. Johnny had stopped to cut himself a stick and had wandered a little way off course.

Now he was sitting in his seat and digging into his rucksack.

Suddenly he looked up and asked, 'Why are you all staring at me like that?'

'What? Oh, nothing,' they said.

Then one of them called out, 'You've got ever such a lot of freckles on your nose!' — And they all laughed, including Johnny.

'But I've always had those,' he said.

(Re-told from Ursula Wolfel.)

Hymn
I will bring to you the best gift I can offer (*Come and Praise* 59).
I belong to a family, the biggest on earth (*Come and Praise* 69).

CLOSING PRAYER

We join together to say:

May the Lord keep us all in his care; may he watch over those whom we love, and those who love us.

Amen.

Closing music
Quiet, very short piece of music played.
Any necessary announcements.

Recessional music
Children leave whilst appropriate music is played by pianist, group, school orchestra or from a recording.

For younger children
(For involvement before, during or after assembly.)

- Write down the names of your friends.

- Say why you like your best friends.

- Draw or paint a picture of your best friend.

For older children
(For involvement before, during or after assembly.)

- Draw a portrait of one of your friends.

- Write a description of your best friend and list the things you like and dislike about him/her.

- Discuss 'Friendship' and its implications.

- Find out the names of Jesus' disciples.

PEACE

Preparation
If possible have a single specimen (or several in a vase) of the rose called Peace. Alternatively, a picture of the rose could be shown.

Opening music
As the children assemble, music should be played by the school orchestra, a group, or soloist, or from a recording.

GREETING

Leader: 'Good morning children.'

Children: 'Good morning (leader's name); good morning everyone.'
All adults present: 'Good morning children.'

INTRODUCTION

Look at this beautiful rose. It is called 'Peace'. It has lemon yellow petals and edges flushed with pink. It is one of the most famous and popular of roses and today we are going to hear its remarkable story.

When we think about peace we know that throughout history, and even today, wars and fighting have caused great misery and suffering. During the First World War (1914–1918), nearly nine million soldiers were killed. During the second world war (1939–1945), six million Jews were killed in concentration camps.

Peace always brings joy and hope and we remember that Jesus came to bring 'Peace on earth, Goodwill toward men'.

PRAYER

Let us pray for lasting peace throughout the world.

Dear God, please grant that all men and women may be filled with your Holy Spirit — and hate war and love peace. Help all the world's children to learn that it is better to love than to fight — so that all wars may cease and your Kingdom of Love may be established throughout the world.

Amen.

Hymn
Shalom, Shalom (Peace, Peace) (*Come and Praise* 141).
I've got peace like a river (*Come and Praise* 143).
Lead me from death to life (*Come and Praise* 140).

Bible reference
Everlasting Peace, Isaiah ch 2 verse 4.

CONTENT

The Peace rose

In 1935, Monsieur Antoine Meilland, a famous rose grower in France, created a new rose after many years of cultivating various specimens. He decided to dedicate this new rose to the memory of his wife and he carefully nurtured the young trial plants for several years — until the outbreak of the second World War.

In 1941, when the Germans occupied France, they heard about Antoine's new rose and decided to take it from him. He had other ideas. War was the enemy of beauty and to create a rose was the answer to ugliness he said and he planned to smuggle his precious plants out of the country.

Antoine gave the Germans a different rose and took his cuttings and plants to the American Consulate at Lyons. Mr Whittinghill, the American Consul, agreed to take the specimens to the United States.

In America, Mr Whittinghill gave the rose cuttings to Mr Conrad Pyle who lived in Pennsylvania and looked after a plant nursery. Mr Pyle very carefully tended the new rose plants until the end of the war.

On the very day that Berlin was captured by the allies, Monsieur Meilland was told that his rose cuttings had survived and flourished. They had been developed so successfully that they were now ready to be made available to the public.

Antoine was overjoyed to hear that his precious rose had grown healthily. He decided that although he had created the rose in memory of his wife, he sent an urgent message to Pennsylvania, saying, 'Re-name the rose PEACE'.

When delegates arrived in San Francisco from all over the world at the end of the war in 1945 to set up the United Nations, a Peace rose was placed in every delegate's room. By 1951, over one million Peace rose bushes had been bought in this country alone. No other rose has won the hearts of people, and especially gardeners, as the Peace rose — and it is easy to see why.

(Re-told from Betty Patston.)

Hymn
Peace is flowing like a river (*Come and Praise* 144).
Make me a channel of your peace (*Come and Praise* 147).
Peace, perfect peace (*Come and Praise* 53).

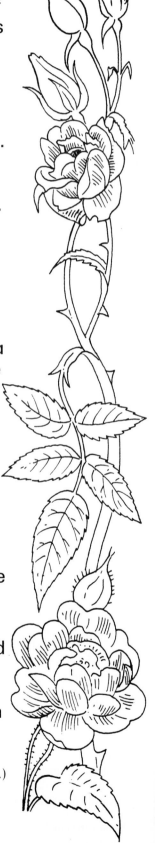

CLOSING PRAYER

May the Prince of Peace lead our thoughts and guide our steps to give peace in our hearts which will help give peace where we live which will help give peace in the world.

Amen.

Closing music
A very short, quiet piece of music is played by the pianist whilst all present spend a few moments in silent reflection. Any necessary announcements.

Recessional music
Appropriate music is played by a soloist, group or orchestra, or from a recording as the children leave.

For younger children
(For involvement before, during or after assembly.)

● Talk about and/or show some summer flowers.

● Make a summer flowers frieze — using pictures cut from seed and flower catalogues or using cut out shapes from coloured gummed paper.

For older children
(For involvement before, during or after assembly.)

● June is known as the 'month of roses'. List the names of some cultivated roses and find out why they were given their names.

● Draw and/or paint a rose from a single specimen.

● Find out about the United Nations Organisation and what it does.

Additional material

Poem
You love the roses — so do I. I wish
The sky would rain down roses, as they rain
From off the shaken bush. Why will it not?
Then all the valley would be pink and white
And soft to tread on. They would fall as light
As feathers, smelling sweet: and it would be
Like sleeping and yet waking, all at once.

George Eliot

SUMMER

Opening music
Music is played by a pianist, group, orchestra or from a recording as the children enter and take their places.

GREETING

Leader: 'Good morning children.'

Children: 'Good morning (leader's name); good morning to all.'
All adults present: 'Good morning children.'

INTRODUCTION

Our assembly today is about summer. Close your eyes for a moment and think about summertime. I wonder which pictures come into your mind's eye? These are some of the pictures I can see:

Children playing on a sunny beach or paddling in the sea.

Holiday picnics and barbecues.

Wild flowers in the hedgerows, green fields and cool leafy woods.

Clear blue skies and hot sunny days.

Outdoor sports and games.

Now, open your eyes and tell me some of the pictures you saw which I have not mentioned.

(Individual children are invited to suggest their ideas.)

Of course not all summer days are fine and warm. It does sometimes rain in England in summer!

Let us say a prayer to thank God for summertime.

PRAYER

We offer our thanks, dear God, for the glory of summertime. We think of the hills and valleys, rivers, woods, moorlands, lanes, meadows and sea shore bathed in the brightness of the summer sunshine. We thank you for calm days; the beauty of earth and sky; the greenness of the countryside and the colouring of the flowers, fruits and trees. Finally, we thank you for holidays and the chance to enjoy playing outdoors in the warmth of the sun and your love.

Amen.

The Lord's prayer (if desired).

Hymn
Morning has broken (*Come and Praise* 1).
All things bright and beautiful (*Come and Praise* 3).

Bible reference
In Praise of the Creator, Psalm 104 vv 10–14 and v 31.

CONTENT

I am sure you have realised that summer days are the longest in the year. Actually, all the days of the year are the same length, but summer days have more hours of sunlight and seem longer. This is an old story about longer summer days.

Long, long ago, at the very beginning of time, the sun used to rush across the sky very quickly. Everyone grumbled because it made the day so short! There wasn't enough time to go hunting and fishing and not enough daylight to do all the work that had to be done. A fisherman called Mani decided that he would teach the sun a lesson. He worked out a plan to slow down the sun so that there would be more hours of daylight.

Mani took his strong fishing net and set out one morning, before dawn. He sailed, in his canoe, to the very edge of the earth where he knew the sun rose from beneath the ocean. As he waited for the sun to rise, he cast his large net over the sea where he thought the sun would come up.

Soon the sun appeared and gradually began to rise but before it knew what was happening, it found itself caught in Mani's net. Mani pulled the ropes of the net tight and the sun stopped rising.

'Why do you race across the sky from east to west and not give us enough time to hunt, fish and do our work?' asked Mani.

'Oh, please let me out of the net. I have a very long journey to make in one day and the seas must be warmed and the crops ripened in all the lands — and I must not be late!' replied the sun.

Mani held on to the net, even though some of the ropes were burning.

'I have an idea', said the sun, 'and if you let me go, I promise to tell you what it is.'

Mani carefully loosened the net but he wisely did not release all the ropes holding the sun in case the sun deceived him. The sun rose higher in the sky and then told Mani about its idea. 'Perhaps, if I stay still and let the earth travel round me instead of me travelling round the earth, you will get your longer days — but only in the summertime,' said the sun.

Mani agreed to this idea and let go of the net which held the sun. He paddled back to his own country as the sun shone down kindly on him.

And that is how it has been to this very day. The ropes of Mani's net may still be seen hanging from the sun when it rises and sets. We call them the sun's rays.

The days are longer in our summertime and the longest day of the year is on 24th June, the day when Mani originally caught the sun in his net and made it stay still in the sky.

(Re-told from A.G. Patston.)

Hymn
For the beauty of the earth (*Come and Praise* 11).
Glad that I live am I.

CLOSING PRAYER

Let us say together:

May the Lord keep us all in his care. May he watch over those whom we love, and those who love us.

Amen.

Closing music
Quiet, very short piece of music is played.
Any necessary announcements.

Recessional music
Children leave assembly whilst appropriate music is played by pianist, group or orchestra, or from a recording.

For younger children
(For involvement before, during or after assembly.)

- Talk about the joys and dangers of summertime.

- Make a summer frieze showing flowers, animals and activities.

- Discuss the seasons and how they vary.

- Find, read, recite and/or learn and/or compose poems about summer.

For older children
(For involvement before, during or after assembly.)

- List some of the festivals and plays etc. associated with summer and possibly perform extracts from one or other of them (e.g. Maypole dance; A Midsummer Night's Dream; Sun God dance drama.)

- Find out and tell or write about Rogationtide (the three days before Ascension Day are known as Rogation Days — 'Asking Days') and 24th June — Birthday of Saint John The Baptist.

- Write and tell about a summer holiday.

Further suggestions

- Discuss and explain the seasons; the earth's orbit around the sun; inclination of the earth.

- Find and sing songs associated with summer.

- Poems and extracts for reading, learning, handwriting practice or illustrating:
  'And what is so rare as a day in June?
  Then, if ever, come perfect days'. (J.R.Lowell.)
  The Months — Sara Coleridge.
  Summer — Christina Rossetti.
  June Wind — Malcolm Hemphrey.

Poem
Summer
First, April, she with mellow showers
Opens the way for early flowers;
Then after her comes smiling May,
In a more sweet and rich array;
Next enters June, and brings us more
Gems than those two who went before:
Then, lastly, July comes, and she
More wealth brings in than all those three.

Robert Herrick

MOONY'S SANDALS

GREETING

Leader: 'Good morning children.'

Children: 'Good morning (leader's name); good morning to all.'
All adults present: 'Good morning children.'

INTRODUCTION

Today we are thinking about children who are disabled. There are some children who cannot hear or see properly. There are some children who cannot walk freely. There are some children who cannot speak clearly. Some girls and boys do not have full control over their body movements. They appear to be clumsy and their movements may seem jerky. We need to understand the needs of children who are disabled. They usually want to be treated normally, without fuss. We must never make fun of children who have difficulty in making themselves understood. We need to be kind, sympathetic and patient when we meet children who, at first, seem different from ourselves.

PRAYER

Lord Jesus we know that most children are full of life and movement and we ask you to bless, help and comfort all those boys and girls who are disabled. Teach those of us who are fit and well to use our strength, intelligence and mobility to assist those who cannot help themselves.

Amen.

The Lord's Prayer (if desired).

Hymn
He gave me eyes so I could see (*Come and Praise* 18).
There is singing in the desert (*Come and Praise* 26).

Bible reference
Jesus heals the man with the useless hand (St Luke ch 6 vv 6–10, selected).
Jesus heals the deaf man (St Mark ch 7 vv 32–37, selected).
Jesus heals the boy with the evil spirit (St Mark ch 9 vv 14–29).

CONTENT

Moony's Sandals

Moony is big; almost as big as the boys who are old enough to ride mopeds. He already has bristles on his chin. But Moony still talks like a small child and loves to play with younger children. They tease him because he cannot speak clearly and his movements are awkward. Some children call out, 'Moony's not right in the head' or say, 'Moony's thick'.

One day Moony was wearing new sandals which he kept stroking. The children started to taunt him. 'Hello stupid!' they yelled. They laughed — and Moony laughed too. He liked it when they talked to him; he didn't understand that they were making fun of him. He tried to talk back to them. His thick tongue forced out '-dals', and he pointed to his new shiny sandals. A girl said, 'Oh! Look, he's dribbling again!'

The children moved on and Moony followed them. He caught hold of a small boy's hand and pulled it down to touch his sandals because he thought the boy would like to stroke them. The boy was frightened and cried out in fear. He kicked out at Moony's leg and screamed. The children gathered round. They pushed Moony off and shouted at him. 'You and your stupid sandals!' they cried. 'Leave him alone, he's smaller then you'. They forced Moony back against the wall and one by one they stood on Moony's feet until his new sandals were dirty and badly scratched. Then a woman arrived. She shouted at the children and told them to leave Moony alone. Moony did not know what was happening but he could tell the woman was angry so when the children ran away, he ran with them.

When he arrived home wheezing and panting, his mother looked down at his feet.

'What have you been doing to your lovely new sandals?' she asked in dismay.

Moony could not explain.

His mother tried to clean and polish them and Moony watched, smiling. But Moony did not want to wear them any more because they were no longer smooth and shining. Moony went into the street again. The children were now riding their bicycles. They skimmed past him as he stood on the edge of the pavement.

'Look out Moony, the sun'll dry out what's left of your pin-sized brain,' a boy shouted. All the children laughed, and Moony laughed too because he enjoyed being with them.

(Re-told from Ursula Wolfel.)

Hymn
Would you walk by on the other side (*Come and Praise* 70).
Heavenly Father, may thy blessing (*Come and Praise* 62).

CLOSING PRAYER

We all join together to say:

May the Lord keep us all in his care; may he watch over those whom we love, and those who love us.

Amen.

Closing music
Quiet, very short piece (few bars), played.
Any necessary announcements.

Recessional music
Children leave at the close of the assembly whilst appropriate music is played by the pianist, group, school orchestra, or from a recording.

For younger or older children
(For involvement before, during or after assembly.)

- Discuss how children who are physically or mentally disabled should be treated.

- Possibly invite children from a 'Special School' to visit, perhaps to see a school production or concert.

- Consider inviting a parent of a disabled child to talk about the problems that can arise within the family and outside the home.

CONTENTMENT

Opening music
Music of an appropriate nature is played by a pianist, group, school orchestra or from a recording as children assemble.

GREETING

Leader: 'Good morning children.'

Children: 'Good morning (leader's name); good morning to all.'
All adults present: 'Good morning children.'

INTRODUCTION

Are you always satisfied with what you have? Do you sometimes wish that you lived in a bigger or better house? Do you sometimes think that your friends are better off than you are? Some people are never content. They always want more or better. Have you heard the expression, 'The grass in the next field always looks greener'? Find out what the saying means.

Our assembly today is about being happy and contented with our own houses and homes. We do not need to live in a palace or a mansion to be happy and satisfied.

Hymn
Glad that I live am I.
Thank you, Lord, for this new day (*Come and Praise* 32).

PRAYER

Let us spend a few moments in silence during which time we can think about, and thank, God for his gifts to us. (Pause).

Heavenly Father, we have so much for which to be thankful — our homes, our families, our friends — and the wonderful world in which we live. Help us not to be envious or discontented but rather to be happy and satisfied with what we have.

Amen.

The Lord's Prayer (if desired).

Bible reference
Trust in God, St Luke ch 12 vv 22–31.

CONTENT

Here is a story about a boy who thought that a house that he often looked at was better than his own. He wished that he could move and live in the house that he admired so much but listen to the story to find out what happened.

The House with the Golden Windows

There once lived a boy named Peter. He lived in a cottage on the side of a hill. His parents were very good to him and he had his own room and a cupboard full of toys. His father, who looked after the garden which was colourful and tidy, built Peter a swing in a quiet shady corner. Peter had a lovely home and parents who loved him. He should have been happy and contented, but every evening, when the sun was low, he used to sit on the step outside the front door with his chin cupped in his hands, and gaze across the valley at the house on the other side.

This house was different from his. It had beautiful golden windows.

Peter never tired of looking at the house with the golden windows. Day after day he stared across at the house on the other side of the valley.

'How lucky the people are who live there,' he thought.

One day in summer Peter made up his mind to see the wonderful house with the windows of gold.

His mother packed a picnic for him and he set out with his eyes firmly fixed on the house across the valley. He could not wait to see the

wonderful house that he had stared at for so long. Peter trudged along the road and it seemed a very long way. On and on he went, down the valley and then up the steep winding hill on the other side. At last, tired and very weary, he arrived at the gate of the house and looked up. What a surprise! What a disappointment! It wasn't a wonderful house with golden windows, it was a cottage just like his own with glass windows.

Peter sat down and ate his picnic. He felt sad and unhappy. He had

52

walked a great distance and the marvellous house with the golden windows did not exist! It was now early evening and Peter prepared to start the journey back to his own house. He looked back across the valley at his own cottage, and a wonderful sight met his eyes. It was a house with golden windows far more beautiful than the one he had seen before. It was his own house, and the sun was shining on the windows just as it had shone on those he had been looking at for years!

Peter returned home a wiser boy than he had been when he set out that morning. He thought, 'if only I had looked at my own windows, I wouldn't have had to come all this way for nothing!'

Do you understand the message of this story?

(Re-told from A.G. Patston.)

Hymn
Join with us to sing God's praises (*Come and Praise* 30).
Now thank we all our God (*Come and Praise* 38).

CLOSING PRAYER

Let us join together to say:

May the Lord keep us all in his care; may he watch over those whom we love, and those who love us.

Amen.

Closing music
The children remain still after the closing prayer whilst the pianist plays a few bars of quiet music.
Any necessary announcements.

Recessional music
The pianist, group, school orchestra or recorded music plays whilst all leave the assembly.

For younger children
(For involvement before, during or after assembly.)

- Act out the story of 'The House With The Golden Windows'.

- Tell or write about the things you like about your home and house.

- Draw and/or paint a picture of your house.

- Write or tell about the members of your family.

For older children
(For involvement before, during or after assembly.)

What I like about my house ....

- Write and read or recite a poem entitled 'Contentment'.

- Discuss why envy may lead to jealousy (e.g. the story of Joseph).

- Consider these sayings and quotes:

    'Keeping up with the Jones's'.
    'I had no shoes and complained, until I met a man who had no feet' (Chinese proverb).
    'Yes, we have a home, but no house to put round it!' (Child refugee).
    'Enough is as good as a feast'.
    'The camel, desiring horns, lost its ears as well' (Latin proverb).

SHADOWS

Opening music
As the children assemble, music is played by a pianist, group, school orchestra or from a recording.

GREETING

Leader: 'Good morning children.'

Children: 'Good morning (leader's name); good morning everybody.'
All adults present: 'Good morning children.'

INTRODUCTION

Sunny days in September are particularly beautiful. Have you noticed the long dark shadows in September? Why are the shadows so long and distinct in September?

(Pause for answers.)

In our assembly today we are thinking about sunshine and shadows — particularly shadows.

Hymn
God who made the earth (*Come and Praise* 10).
Morning has broken (*Come and Praise* 1).

PRAYER

O God of all comfort, help us to face joys and sorrows in the certain knowledge that you are with us both on good days and bad days, happy days and sad days. Help us particularly, to face difficulties and sadness with strength and faith.

Amen.

The Lord's prayer (if desired).

Bible reference
Trust in God, Psalm 56 vv 2–3. St John ch 14 v 27.

CONTENT

The Man Who Sold His Shadow

There once lived a young man named John who, because he wanted to be rich and famous, seemed always to be dissatisfied and miserable with his life. One fine September day, when the sun was casting particularly long shadows everywhere, John was stopped by a merchant. 'You have a fine long shadow following you, young man,' said the merchant.

'Have I?' replied John. 'Well the sun is low in the sky and September is the month of long shadows,' he added.

'I am buying shadows,' the merchant went on, 'and I would like to buy yours.'

John thought the man was joking so he said, 'Well, I don't think my shadow is much use to me. What will you pay me for it?' The merchant thought for a moment, then he said, 'I haven't much money at the present time, but if you will sign this paper saying that I can have your shadow, I will promise to make you rich and famous.'

John was pleased to think that he would be rich and famous so he signed the paper. The merchant took a pair of scissors and, bending down, he cut off John's shadow close to his heels. He then rolled up the shadow, stuffed it into a bag and, with a strange chuckle he raised his hat in thanks and hurried away.

From that very day John became very rich and everything he touched turned to gold. At first he did not miss his shadow as he quickly became famous and the envy of all his friends. Then, slowly, people began to notice.

'That's strange,' they muttered, 'the sun is shining and yet John has no shadow. Why can that be?' And they began to whisper among themselves and nudge each other when John walked by.

John began to notice what was happening and how people avoided him. He began to feel very uncomfortable and missed his shadow. Sometimes he would jump round quickly to see if had returned. Alas, the shadow was never there.

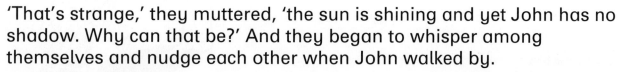

John now began to stay indoors if the sun was shining and then he grew nervous and even stayed indoors on dull and cloudy days.

Finally, John could stand it no longer.

He found the merchant who had bought his shadow and begged him to return it. 'Yes,' agreed the merchant, 'but only if you give me the riches you have gained and everything that you possess.'

John agreed.

When the merchant gave him back his shadow he said, 'Remember, young man, that shadows, as well as sunshine, are a part of our lives.'

(Re-told from A.G. Patston.)

Hymn
Fill your hearts with joy and gladness (*Come and Praise* 9).
Can you be sure that the rain will fall? (*Come and Praise* 31).

CLOSING PRAYER

Let us say together:

May the Lord keep us all in his care; may he watch over those whom we love, and those who love us.

Amen.

Closing music
A short piece is played (by the pianist?) whilst all remain silent and still.
Any necessary announcements.

Recessional music
An appropriate piece is played by the pianist, group, school orchestra or from a recording as all leave.

For younger children
(For involvement before, during or after the assembly.)

● On a sunny day, stand in the playground and ask a friend to trace round your shadow. Mark the place where you stand. Later, return to the same place and ask your friend to trace round your shadow again. (This exercise could be carried out at regular intervals during the day.) Notice how your shadow seems to move round and change in length.

● Make a shadow theatre and use shadow puppets to act out a story.

For older children
(For involvement before, during or after assembly.)

● On a sunny day use a metre stick to cast a shadow. Mark the shadow length and direction at regular intervals during the day.

● Find out why the shadow changes length and direction. Discuss the reason for the changes.

● Construct a simple sun dial.

- Make and use shadow puppets. (A sheet as a screen with a rear source of light will be required.)

- Make a classroom frieze using silhouettes. (Black silhouettes on white are most effective.)

- Using the shadow created by shining a light (e.g. a torch or projector lamp), trace round your friend's head profile on to black or dark coloured paper. Cut out the silhouette. All the class can be involved and all the head silhouettes could be mounted as pictures or on a frieze. (The children could guess each other's names from the silhouettes.)

Additional material

Poem
My Shadow
I have a little shadow that goes in and out with me,
And what can be the use of him is more than I can see.
He is very, very like me from the heels up to the head;
And I see him jump before me, when I jump into my bed.

The funniest thing about him is the way he likes to grow —
Not at all like proper children, which is always very slow;
For he sometimes shoots up taller, like an indiarubber ball,
And he sometimes gets so little that there's none of him at all.

He hasn't got a notion of how children ought to play,
And can only make a fool of me in every sort of way.
He stays so close beside me, he's a coward you can see;
I'd think shame to stick to nursie as that shadow sticks to me!

One morning, very early, before the sun was up,
I rose and found the shining dew on every buttercup;
But my lazy little shadow, like an errant sleepy-head,
Had stayed at home behind me and was fast asleep in bed.

Robert Louis Stevenson

PLANTING BULBS

Preparation

Have ready to hand on a small table: some hyacinth bulbs, bulb fibre, water in a small watering can (or similar), a clean cloth, a bulb pot, some pieces of broken pot (or similar). (If desired a second bulb pot and other bulbs for indoor flowering could be made available).

Opening music

As the children assemble, music by a pianist, group, school orchestra or from a recording should be played.

GREETING

Leader: 'Good morning children.'

Children: 'Good morning (leader's name); good morning to all.'
All adults present: 'Good morning children.'

INTRODUCTION

Autumn is a busy time for gardeners. Many plants are dying after flowering throughout the summer and flower beds have to be cleared and dug at this time of year. It is also the time when bulbs are planted outdoors and indoors for spring flowering. In our assembly this morning we are actually going to plant some bulbs which we hope will flower indoors next spring.

Hymn

All things bright and beautiful (*Come and Praise* 3).
I planted a seed (*Come and Praise* 134).

PRAYER

Dear God, maker of all that is beautiful in this world, we praise you for colour, scent, softness and strength. Especially today we thank you for the wonderful flowers that emerge from bulbs. Help us to take proper care of the bulbs we are about to plant so that we can help you in your lovely handiwork.

Amen.

The Lord's Prayer (if desired).

CONTENT

Put up your hands and tell me the names of some spring flowering bulbs.

(Snowdrops, crocuses, daffodils, narcissus, etc.)
(Hold up a hyacinth bulb)

What is the name of this bulb? It looks like an onion! (A white or purple onion). It is a hyacinth bulb. Can you spell its name? Call out:
H - Y - A - C - I - N - T - H.

Do you know the name of the special kind of soil in which we should we plant indoor bulbs?

(Answers may include, dirt, earth, fertilizer, compost, peat, manure, etc.)

It is called 'fibre' — F - I - B - R - E.

Now I should like two of you to come out and help plant our bulbs this morning.

(Choose two children — possibly an infant and a junior child. The two children are introduced by the leader who now addresses them.)

Would you first of all place some of the broken pieces of pots in the bottom of the pot we are going to use.

Why should we place broken pieces of pots or stones in the bottom? Do you think we are we going to try to grow pots!?

(Answer required — the stones or broken pieces of pots will give good drainage and prevent the bulbs becoming too wet which may cause them to rot.)

Now place some fibre in the pot, to cover the drainage pieces. The fibre needs to half fill the pot.

Now you need to plant the hyacinth bulbs. Rest each, in turn, on the fibre in the pot. Which way up should we plant them?

(Hold up a bulb. Point it upwards, then downwards and then sideways. It is hoped the children watching will decide which is the right way up for the bulbs!)

I wonder what would happen if we planted the bulb upside-down or pointing sideways?

(In fact, the bulb would probably right itself by using its growing roots to pull itself the right way round.)

Now add more fibre to fill the pot. The tips of the bulbs should be showing just above the top of the fibre.

(The two children should complete this task and then use the cloth to wipe their hands.)

Finally, what do you think we need to add?

(Water. Ask one of the two children to water the newly planted bulbs.)

These bulbs should now be placed in a cool, dark place for several weeks. This will encourage the roots to grow. The fibre should be kept moist, but not too wet. When the bulbs begin to send up their shoots we can take the pot out of the dark and place it where we wish to see the flowers bloom.

We look forward to seeing our bulbs flower in the spring. Perhaps you would like to plant some bulbs of your own at home or in your classroom.

Hymn
Autumn days when the grass is jewelled (*Come and Praise* 4).
The earth is yours, O God (*Come and Praise* 6).

CLOSING PRAYER

Let us join together to say:

May the Lord keep us all in his care; may he watch over those whom we love, and those who love us.

Amen.

Closing music
The pianist plays a few bars of quiet music whilst all present remain quiet and still.
Any necessary announcements.

Recessional music
As the children leave the assembly, music is played by the pianist, group, school orchestra or from a recording.

For younger children
(For involvement before, during or after assembly.)

- Plant pots of indoor bulbs (various kinds).

- Collect pictures of spring flowering bulbs, stick on a frieze and name.

- Plant bulbs outdoors in the school grounds if possible. (A group of snowdrops or crocuses under a nearby tree?)

- Plant some specially prepared bulbs for Christmas flowering.

For older children
(For involvement before, during or after assembly.)

- Plant individual or group pots of indoor bulbs. Record the planting procedure carefully — with illustrations.

- Plant a single hyacinth bulb in a hyacinth pot (in order to see the root system develop later).

- Plant outdoor bulbs in the school grounds if possible (e.g. daffodils for naturalising).

- Assume responsibility for part of the school grounds (e.g. cultivate an area as a class garden; build a simple rockery; design and construct a school pond; create a conservation area).

- Discuss — what makes the bulb grow? Who 'puts life' into a seemingly dead-looking bulb?

HARVEST

Preparation

A display of harvest produce could be arranged before the assembly. A harvest picture or frieze could be mounted behind the tables of flowers, fruit, vegetables etc. A harvest loaf, and possibly a glass of water, a lump of coal and a fresh fish may be used as a centre-piece. It is suggested that each child should be invited to bring one item for the harvest display. Tinned items could be encouraged as the persons receiving the harvest goods may appreciate items that can be stored.

If desired one spare table should be placed at the front on which could be placed token gifts; these gifts to be brought out by two children from each class, either at the beginning of the assembly as each class arrives — or during the singing of the first hymn. The gifts could be received by the leader or a parent, governor or other visiting guest.

Seven children should be chosen beforehand to sit at the front. Each of these children should have a large letter on card measuring approximately 45 cm × 30 cm (or smaller if desired). The letters are H A R V E S T. The children do not hold up the letters until told to do so in the assembly. On the backs of the cards are written the following numbers (so that the children holding up the letters can see them, but the assembly children cannot).

H - 1, A - 2, R - 3, V - 4, E - 5, S - 6, T - 7.

Each of the seven children needs to know the number on his/her card and must stand up and display his/her letter when his/her number is called by the leader.

Opening music

Appropriate music is played by the pianist, group, school orchestra or from a recording as the children assemble.

GREETING

Leader: 'Good morning children.'

Children: 'Good morning (leader's name); good morning to all.'
All adults present: 'Good morning children.'

INTRODUCTION

Today we are celebrating our Harvest Festival. First, I should like you all just to look at all the lovely gifts of flowers, fruit and vegetables on display.

(Pause for children to look.)

One other thing you may have noticed is the lovely smell of Harvest Festival produce. Thank you all for bringing your harvest gifts, and please thank your parents for providing them. After our assembly, all the flowers, fruit and vegetables will be taken to (?).

(Mention the planned distribution arrangements — whether children will be involved etc.)

Look at the lovely Harvest Loaf (describe it). Later this morning we shall cut up the loaf and all the children in Year 1 (or substitute name of youngest class) will each be given a piece to eat.

Hymn
The earth is yours, O God (*Come and Praise* 6).
Let us with a gladsome mind (*Come and Praise* 8).
(Token gifts may be brought up from each class during the hymn.)

PRAYER

Father, we thank and praise you for the wonder of harvest time. For the corn of the field and the fruit of the orchard, for the harvest of the sea and the treasures of the mines we give you thanks. May we, who have plenty, remember those in need. Teach us never to waste your gifts but use and share them for the sake of our Lord Jesus Christ.

Amen.

The Lord's Prayer (if desired).

Bible reference
Praise and Thanksgiving, Psalm 65 vv 9–13.
God's Promise, Genesis ch 8 v 22.

CONTENT

The seven children who are sitting in front of you each has a letter. They will now stand up and hold up their letters. What word does it say? (H A R V E S T).

(The seven children sit down in between the words, then stand up again when their number is called.)

God's wonderful gifts of food come to us from the (call out 5 2 3 7 1) (E A R T H), or from the 6 5 2 (S E A).

The amount of food in the world is 4 2 6 7 (V A S T).

Whilst we all have enough to 5 2 7 (E A T).

We must remember that in some countries, because of famine and drought many people 6 7 2 3 4 5 (S T A R V E).

I am sure you would agree that we must learn to 6 1 2 3 5 (S H A R E).

I hope you will remember this Harvest Festival and the important messages — that we need to say thank you for all God's goodness and gifts to us and that we need to share what we have with others.

Hymn
When God made the hamper of creation (*Come and Praise* 16).
Autumn days when the grass is jewelled (*Come and Praise* 4).

CLOSING PRAYER

We join together to say:

May the Lord keep us all in his care; may he watch over those whom we love, and those who love us.

Amen.

Closing music
The pianist plays a few bars of quiet music whilst all remain still and quiet.
Any necessary announcements.

Recessional music
Music is played by the pianist, group, school orchestra or from a recording as all the children leave the assembly.

For younger children
(For involvement before, during or after assembly.)

● Cut out shapes of fruits or vegetables to stick on a colourful harvest wall mural.

● Use the word HARVEST to compose an acrostic poem.

● Prepare and display two meals — one very large using foods that are available to us in this country and one very meagre (just a small quantity of rice?) to show the difference between the Western and Third World provision.

For older children
(For involvement before, during or after assembly.)

● Organise a class, year or school competition making as many words as possible from the word HARVEST.

● Find out about: harvest times in other lands; other countries' produce (e.g. rice, grain, fruit, coffee etc.); climate and crops inter-dependence; modern and earlier traditional harvesting methods. Who or what were 'gleaners'?

- Read the story of Ruth (the book of Ruth ch 2).
- Find poems about Harvest.

Additional material

The Feast of Tabernacles (the most important ancient Israelite feast).

This marked the beginning of the Jewish year and the time for the celebration of the harvest of grapes, figs and olives. During the harvesting period in the orchards and vineyards, many workers built temporary shelters called 'Booths' or 'Sukkahs', and slept outside in them.

A simple Sukkah could be built for assembly as a harvest centre-piece. (Timber frame or table on its side; roof of branches interlaced with foliage; sides covered with green paper; inside decorated with pictures and hung with flowers and fruit.) Traditional offerings were citron, palm, myrtle and willow but children could bring their own offerings to hang in the Sukkah.

THE SEA

Preparation

A display entitled 'The Sea' could be mounted. It could include such items as a large draped net and cork or glass floats, cut out fish shapes (possibly made by the children), shells of all shapes and sizes, smooth stones, cut out or real strands of sea weed, a lobster pot, a bucket and spade, model ships etc.

The display could be backed by a large wall mural or collage prepared by the children if desired.

Opening music

Appropriate music is played by the pianist, group, school orchestra or from a recording as the children enter.

GREETING

Leader: 'Good morning children.'

Children: 'Good morning (leader's name); good morning everyone.'
All adults present: 'Good morning children.'

INTRODUCTION

Today our assembly is about the sea. The sea, like many of us, has different moods. Sometimes it is quiet, placid, still and calm whilst on other occasions it can be rough, boisterous, noisy and dangerous. We must never underestimate the power of the sea and even when it appears peaceful and inviting we must always treat it with care and respect.

What kind of games and activities do you enjoy at the sea-side? What happens when you build a huge sandcastle or a wall of sand round a hole, deep enough to crouch in, when the tide comes in? No doubt most of you enjoy visiting the sea-side and playing on the sands, paddling or swimming in the sea or exploring the wonderful rock pools with all their exciting sea life treasures.

PRAYER

Let us say a prayer about the sea.

Dear God, who made the seas and oceans and all the creatures that live in them, take care of sailors and fishermen; those who go down to the sea in ships and work upon the great waters. Be with the lighthouse keepers, the pilots and those who risk their lives in lifeboats. Let us remember the prayer of the Breton fishermen: 'Dear God, be good to me. The sea is so wide and my boat is so small.'

Amen.

The Lord's prayer (if desired).

Hymn
In the morning early (*Come and Praise* 60).
Little drops of water.

Bible reference
The great catch of fish, St Luke ch 5 vv 1–11.
God's goodness to fishermen, Psalm 107 vv 23–30.

CONTENT

Listen to a story re-told from St Mark's Gospel about the time that Jesus was caught in a sudden storm when sailing on the sea.

Storm on the Sea of Galilee

It was early evening when Jesus, who had been preaching and teaching all day, arrived on the shore of the Sea of Galilee. Jesus was tired but he continued to teach as he sat in one of the boats which was pulled up on the sandy beach. The great crowd of people stood and listened eagerly as he spoke.

Many of Jesus' special friends were expert fishermen and when Jesus had finished talking to the people, he asked them to ferry him across to the other side. As Jesus and his disciples set out, some of the listening crowd clambered in other boats and tried to follow. The disciples quickly hoisted the triangular sail and steered for the opposite shore. As Jesus was exhausted after his day of teaching and healing, he stretched himself out in the back of the boat and soon fell asleep.

There is no twilight in the East and the night comes suddenly. The other boats had returned to the beach; the waves gently lapped against the side of the boat; a few lights from the lakeside villages gleamed in the darkness and the stars twinkled overhead. The disciples spoke in whispers in order not to disturb Jesus.

The boat was a long way from the shore when, suddenly, the wind began to howl and dark clouds blotted out the night sky. Peter was afraid as the winds screeched and great waves began to break over the boat. The sail was torn and the boat began to pitch and toss. Soon it would surely overturn.

All this time Jesus slept but finally the disciples called out in fear.

'Master!' they yelled, 'the boat is sinking and we shall soon drown! Do you not care?'

Then Jesus stood up and, speaking to the storm and the sea, he called out, 'Hush! Be still!'

At once the great storm died down; the wind dropped and the sea became calm. Jesus turned to his disciples and said, 'Why are you such cowards? Have you no faith, even now?' The disciples were quite overcome with wonder and they whispered to one another, saying, 'Who can this man be whom even the winds and waves obey?'

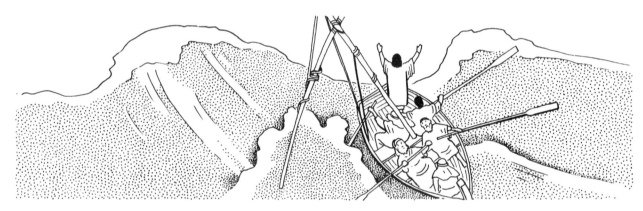

Hymn
Waves are beating on the shore (*Come and Praise* 84).
Spirit of God, as strong as the wind (*Come and Praise* 63).

CLOSING PRAYER

Let us talk to God:
The storm is calmed, the winds die down
Obedient to your will;
The sea that roars, at your command,
— At your command is still.
In midst of danger, fear or death,
Your goodness we'll adore;
And praise you for your mercies past,
And humbly hope for more.

(Adapted from J. Addison, 1672–1719)

And now may the Lord keep us all in his care; may he watch over those whom we love, and those who love us.
Amen.

Closing music

The pianist plays a few bars of music, quietly.
Any necessary announcements.

Recessional music

Children leave at the close of assembly whilst appropriate music is played by the pianist, group, school orchestra or from a recording.

For younger children

(For involvement before, during or after assembly.)

- Act out the story of 'The Stilling of the Tempest'.

- Make a sea shore display in the classroom or hall.

- Make fish mobiles.

- Make a class visit to the seaside.

For older children

(For involvement before, during or after assembly.)
- Invite a member of a life-boat crew to come and talk.
- Construct a model lighthouse with a flashing light.
- Find, write out and learn/recite poems about the sea (e.g. 'Sea Fever' by John Masefield, 'The Sea Shell' by Joyce Winbolt, 'The Sea' by E.M. Adams).
- Find the story about Grace Darling and her brave rescue in 1838 of shipwrecked passengers from the S.S. Forfarshire.

Other suggestions

Play music which has sea connections (e.g. *Fingal's Cave Overture* by Mendelssohn) and use for dance drama and/or movement sequence. Use a length of blue material, raised and lowered to simulate the sea's waves; tie ribbons to children's wrists to simulate wind and spray as they move/dance.

Additional material

An old, amusing quotation from an Arran fisherman, source unknown: 'A man who is not afraid of the sea will soon be drowned for he will be going out on a day he shouldn't. But we do be afraid of the sea and we do only be drowned now and again.'

AUTUMN

Preparation
An autumn display could be prepared, perhaps backed by a wall frieze or large collage on which children's work has been mounted.

Opening music
Appropriate music is played by the pianist, group, school orchestra or from a recording as the children assemble.

GREETING

Leader: 'Good morning children.'

Children: 'Good morning (leader's name); good morning to all.'
All adults present: 'Good morning children.'

INTRODUCTION

Our assembly today is about autumn.

Autumn is a beautiful and colourful season and in our assembly we are going to think about some of the sights and changes that occur at this time of the year. Let us begin by singing an autumn hymn.

Hymn
Autumn days when the grass is jewelled (*Come and Praise* 4).
When from the sky (*Come and Praise* 132).

PRAYER

Lord, we thank you for all the work you do to make this world beautiful. Especially today we thank you for the wonderful signs of autumn, many of which are colourful and glorious to see. We think of the red, brown and yellow-gold leaves which lie in drifted heaps; the bright scarlet berries; seeds and fruits which ripen and the many flowers that make the gardens so pretty in the autumn sunshine.

Amen.

The Lord's prayer (if desired).

Bible reference
Praise and Thanksgiving, Psalm 65 vv 9–13.

CONTENT

A class of children was asked to make a list of The Signs of Autumn. Here is the list the children compiled. Would you have thought of all of these?

- Ripening fruits and seeds — hips from the wild rose, haws on the hawthorn tree, conkers from the horse chestnut tree, apples, pears, acorns from the oak tree, plums, beech nuts, 'helicopter' seeds from the sycamore, blackberries and hazel nuts.

- Morning mists — heavy dew on the grass and on the wonderful spiders' webs. Some of the spiders have beautiful markings.

- Falling leaves — from deciduous trees. The spectacular different leaves make colourful drifted heaps and a multi-coloured carpet which rustles as we run through it in our games.

- Birds migrating — swifts and swallows gather together in flocks as they get ready to fly to warmer countries before winter comes. You can see them lining up on telegraph wires.

- Fungi — at this time of year you can see toadstools and mushrooms. Some are very unusual and some are poisonous so it is better not to touch them but just look and admire their shape and colour. They are quite fascinating.

- Animals hibernating — some creatures sleep during the winter months. Tortoises, dormice, some squirrels, frogs and toads, hedgehogs and snakes hibernate at this time. Squirrels often bury nuts in autumn and then try to find them for food during the winter. Bats hang upside down from roofs of caves and look like umbrellas as they sleep.

- Gardeners are busy in autumn. They clear up the fallen leaves, have bonfires, dig the garden and plant bulbs. The chrysanthemums, Michaelmas daisies, annual flowers and dahlias are particularly colourful in autumn before the frosts come.

Can you think of any other signs of autumn?

Hymn
Michaelmas daisies purple in the border (*Come and Praise* 137).
God who made the earth (*Come and Praise* 10).

CLOSING PRAYER

We join together to say:

May the Lord keep us all in his care; may he watch over those whom we love, and those who love us.

Amen.

Closing music
The pianist plays a few bars of music whilst all stay quiet.
Any necessary announcements.

Recessional music
As the children leave, music is played by the pianist, group, school orchestra or from a recording.

For younger children
(For involvement before, during or after assembly.)

- Make a collection of leaves, seeds or berries, etc.

- Use a variety of seeds to make patterns or seed mosaic pictures.

- Find books about 'Signs of Autumn' and discuss them.

- Find, learn and recite poem(s) about autumn.

For older children
(For involvement before, during or after assembly.)

- Find out about religious festivals that occur during the months of autumn (September, October and November).

- Compare different poems which have been written about autumn (e.g. 'The Garden in September' by Robert Bridges, 'Autumn Leaves' by M.G. Haskins, 'Autumn' by W.B. Rands, etc.).

- Compose an acrostic poem from the word AUTUMN.

- Make up an autumn dance/drama using suitable music (e.g. Rossini: 'Dawn' from the William Tell Overture; Vivaldi: extract from The Seasons).

Additional material

Poem
Falling Leaves
The leaves had a wonderful frolic,
They danced to the wind's loud song,
They whirled, and they floated, and scampered,
They circled and flew along.

'The North Wind is calling, is calling,
And we must whirl round and round,
And then when our dancing is ended
We'll make a warm quilt for the ground.'

J. M. MacDougall Ferguson

The above poem could be read or recited against very quiet background music whilst a group of small children 'act out' the poem in movement.

THE MASTERPIECE

Opening music
Music is played by a pianist, group, school orchestra or from a recording as the children assemble.

GREETING

Leader: 'Good morning children.'

Children: 'Good morning (leader's name); good morning everybody.'
All adults present: 'Good morning children.'

INTRODUCTION

I am sure you would agree that we should always help people who are in need. Some people find it hard not to think of themselves all the time. It is easy to be selfish and think only of ourselves. It is far harder to consider other people, and sometimes it means we must make sacrifices to do so. Today's assembly is about three artists, two of whom helped the third who was in special need.

PRAYER

Let us close our eyes and listen to John Wesley's prayer:
Do all the good you can
By all the means you can,
In all the ways you can,
In all the places you can,
At all the times you can,
To all the people that you can,
As long as ever you can.
Amen.

The Lord's prayer (if desired).

Hymn
When I needed a neighbour, were you there (*Come and Praise* 65).
Heavenly Father, may thy blessing (*Come and Praise* 62).

Bible reference
Love for one another, St John ch 15 vv 12–13.
The Great Commandment, St Matthew ch 22 vv 37–39.

CONTENT

Here is the story of the three poor artists.

There once lived three poor artists in an old, dark, damp terraced house in a slum area of London.

They had very little money and scraped a living by selling a few paintings, now and then, from a pavement pitch nearby.

The oldest of the artists, Mr Kramer, was an Austrian who had come to England many years before, thinking that he would make a fortune. He was now seventy-five years old and crippled with rheumatism. He occupied the downstairs part of the house and had an artist's easel set up in the corner of his room. He said that one day he would paint a masterpiece — but his canvas had been on the easel for twenty five years!

The two other artists, Samantha and Josephine, known as Sam and Jo, were both very young. They were very close friends.

Now one day Jo fell ill. Within a few days her strength seemed to leave her and she lay in her bed, deathly pale and hardly able to speak. Sam was very worried and called the doctor who examined Jo.

'I am afraid your friend has pneumonia,' he explained to Sam.

'She would normally recover from this illness but unfortunately she does not appear to have the will to live. It is vital that she should want to get better.'

Samantha cried bitterly after the doctor had left. However, when she went into Jo's room, she tried to cheer up her friend.

'I will bring you some nice hot soup', she declared.

Jo did not reply but a few minutes later, Sam heard her counting aloud — backwards!

'Nine, eight, seven, six, five,' whispered Jo as she lay in bed gazing out of the window.

'What on earth are you looking at, and what are you counting?' asked Sam.

'I am counting the leaves on the old ivy which is clinging to that brick wall across the courtyard,' said Jo.

'Why?' asked Samantha, who was puzzled by her friend's interest in the bedraggled plant.

74

'Well, you see, I do not want to live. I am counting the leaves which are left on the old ivy. When the last one drops, then I will die.'

Sam was horrified and quickly drew the curtains. With a false bright manner she told Jo not to think such foolish thoughts and quickly left the room.

Sam did not know what to do. She felt so helpless and hurried downstairs to tell old Mr Kramer about Jo and the ivy leaves.

Mr Kramer listened carefully. He said that Jo must regain the will to live.

'She always said that one day she wished to paint in the Lake District, just as one day I will paint my masterpiece,' the old man said as he pondered the situation. Then he told Sam not to give up hope.

That evening Jo insisted on seeing the ivy leaves. Sam pulled back the curtain. There were two leaves left. The wind was rising and a storm was forecast for the night. As they watched, one of the leaves was torn from the ivy.

'Now there is only one leaf left,' murmured Jo. 'The gale tonight will surely snatch the last leaf from its stalk, and tomorrow I will die.'

Sam did not sleep much that night. The wind screamed loudly and the rain lashed the house. The next morning, Jo asked for the curtains to be pulled back. With trembling hands Sam drew them apart.

Both Jo and Sam had a shock when they saw that the one leaf was still alive and clinging to its stem on the thick ivy stalk.

The next day it still survived and Jo looked at it with a studied gaze.

'You know Sam, I believe that leaf has brought me a message of hope. It is not time for me to die.' Jo sat up and almost smiled.

Sam was overjoyed to see the change in her friend. She called the doctor who now seemed much more hopeful when he spoke to her.

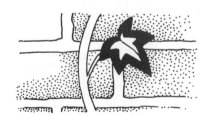

'Your Jo has turned the corner. I believe she will recover quite quickly now. She has regained her will to live. It is a pity, however, that your good friend Mr Kramer will not recover. He was taken into hospital this morning and is not expected to live.' Sam was shocked and saddened to hear this news.

The doctor went on, 'When Mr Kramer was found he was wet through and shivering. Beside him were his palette, brushes and a lantern. A ladder was propped against his door. It would appear that he had been out all night in the violent storm painting an ivy leaf on a brick wall!' Sam thanked the doctor then told Jo the sad news about Mr Kramer.

'Now I know why the last leaf did not fall when the wind blew,' said Jo.

'Perhaps Mr Kramer did paint his masterpiece after all,' remarked Sam.

(Story based on The Last Leaf by O. Henry.)

Hymn
Would you walk by on the other side (*Come and Praise* 70).
Father, hear the prayer we offer (*Come and Praise* 48).

CLOSING PRAYER

Let us say together:

May the Lord keep us all in his care; may he watch over those whom we love, and those who love us.

Amen.

Closing music
Whilst all remain silent and still, the pianist plays a few bars of quiet music.
Any necessary announcements.

Recessional music
As the children leave the assembly, music is played by the pianist, group, school orchestra or from a recording.

For younger children
(For involvement before, during or after assembly.)

- Paint a picture of a leaf and cut it out. (Make a class leaf-frieze using different leaf shapes.)

- Using different coloured paints, make leaf prints. (Cut out and stick on a frieze?)

- Suggest ways in which you can help people who are in need.

For older children
(For involvement before, during or after assembly.)

- Select a leaf and draw it in great detail — using pencil only.

- Take a piece of ivy (with several leaves) then draw and paint what you see. Try to match the colours accurately.

- Find stories of great courage involving people who risked or gave their lives for the sake of others (e.g. Father Damien, Captain Oates).

- Find pictures of masterpieces by famous artists.

FOOD

GREETING

Leader: 'Good morning children.'

Children: 'Good morning (leader's name); good morning to all.'
All adults present: 'Good morning children.'

INTRODUCTION

Our assembly today is about food. We all have to eat to keep ourselves alive and to help us grow. How many of you had breakfast before you came to school today?

Some people eat too much! Some people eat the wrong kinds of food. Some people do not have enough to eat. I wonder which foods you most enjoy eating? Close your eyes for a moment and think about your favourite foods.

(Pause)

Open your eyes. What do you most enjoy eating? What food do you not like eating? I wonder if you know which are healthy foods and which are unhealthy foods. It is important for us to consider a balanced diet which means eating the right amounts of the different kinds of food.

Let us say a prayer about food.

PRAYER

Dear God, we thank you for your good gift of food. Help us never to be wasteful. Teach us to be willing to share our food with those who are hungry. We also thank you for your gift of clear, cool water which quenches our thirst. Give us thankful hearts for all your gifts and goodness to us. Amen.

The Lord's prayer (if desirable).

Hymn
Thank you, Lord, for this new day (*Come and Praise* 32).
Praise the Lord in the rhythm of your music (*Come and Praise* 33).

Bible reference
Jesus Feeds Five Thousand, St Matthew ch 14 vv 15–21.
Elijah fed by the ravens, 1 Kings ch 17 vv 2–6.
Manna (food) from Heaven, Exodus chapter 16.

CONTENT

A teacher once asked the children in her class to make a list of the things they liked to eat, and a list of the things they did not enjoy eating. Here are some of the results:

Peter

My favourite food is fish and chips.

The thing I don't like is liver.

Lucy

I like to eat a Big Mac and tomato ketchup sandwiches.

Custard does not agree with me!

Graham

I like a ploughman's with plenty of cheddar cheese and pickle.

Curry burns my tongue and I don't eat it.

Sylvia

Black forest gateau is my favourite.

I eat cabbage but I don't like it.

Gwyn

The food I enjoy most is fried egg and bacon sandwiches.

I can't think of anything I don't like!

I wonder what you would write down on your lists of 'Food likes and dislikes'?

Hymn
Have you heard the raindrops drumming on the roof-tops? (*Come and Praise* 2).
The earth is yours, O God (*Come and Praise* 6).

CLOSING PRAYER

We say together:

May the Lord keep us all in his care; may he watch over those whom we love, and those who love us.

Amen.

Closing music
Quiet, very short piece of music played by pianist.
Any necessary announcements.

Recessional music
Children leave at the close of the assembly whilst music is played by the pianist, group, school orchestra or from a recording.

For younger children
(For involvement before, during or after assembly.)

- Talk about favourite foods. (Draw and/or paint pictures of favourite meals.)

- Make a class picture showing the children's favourite foods.

- List foods associated with special occasions (e.g. hot cross buns, pancakes).

- Make bread (under adult supervision).

For older children
(For involvement before, during or after assembly.)

- Find out about, and make lists of, healthy foods.

- Research what makes a good diet.

- Why are some foods, if eaten in excess, not good for you?

- List meals and their usual times (e.g. lunch, brunch, dinner, tea, high-tea, evening meal, supper, breakfast etc.). Which foods are eaten by people in other countries?

Further suggestions

- Learn and sing 'Food, glorious food!' (from *Oliver* by Lionel Bart).

- Invite the school's kitchen manager, or other qualified person, to give a brief talk on 'A Balanced Diet'.

- Other possible associated topics — eating sweets (effect on teeth); chips with everything! different kinds of loaves of bread, various kinds of drinks.

Quotes
'Give us this day our daily bread' (Lord's Prayer).
Jesus said, 'I am the bread of life' (St John ch 6 v 35 and v 48).
Jesus said, 'Man cannot live by bread alone'. (St Luke ch 4 v 4).
Man is what he eats (German proverb).

Food and Religions

- Christianity — The significance of sharing bread and wine during the Service of Holy Communion.

- Hinduism — Many Hindus fast one day a week. Many Hindus do not eat meat. (Cows are thought to be sacred in parts of India.)

- Islam — Muslims do not drink alcohol. Muslims must never eat pork and may only eat Halal meat from animals which have been slaughtered ritually.

- Judaism — All food must be prepared according to Jewish law (Kosher). Jews may only eat the flesh of cloven-hoofed animals e.g. cows, sheep, which must be killed in a special way. They may not eat pigs or rabbits. Milk and meat dishes may not be prepared at the same time or eaten at the same meal. Only fish with scales and fins may be eaten.

- Sikhism — Each Sikh Temple or Gurdwara has a kitchen attached. At services a meal called the langar is served for anyone who attends. Sikhs drink a ceremonial drink called Amrit made from sugar crystals at Festival times. Sikhs will only eat meat from animals which are slaughtered humanely. No meat is eaten in the Sikh Temple and many Sikhs are vegetarians.

SISTERS AND BROTHERS

Opening music
As the children assemble, suitable music is played by a pianist, group, school orchestra or from a recording.

GREETING

Leader: 'Good morning children.'

Children: 'Good morning (leader's name): good morning to all.'
All adults present: 'Good morning children.'

INTRODUCTION

Many of you, though not all, have brothers and/or sisters. Family life is precious and although there are sometimes problems, family members love one another.

Hymn
Think of a world without any flowers (*Come and Praise* 17).
I will bring to you the best gift I can offer (*Come and Praise* 59).

PRAYER

Lord Jesus, you know how happy homes can be. Show us how to make our homes full of happiness; teach us to think first of our mothers, fathers, sisters and brothers. When we feel tired and quarrelsome, give us patience. If we feel sulky or spiteful help us to check angry words or actions which could cause conflict and hurt. Help us to show love to all members of our families at all times.

Amen.

Bible reference
Jesus visits Martha and Mary (the two sisters were very different), St Luke ch 10 vv 38–42.
Story of Joseph and his brothers, Genesis chapters 37–47.

CONTENT

Hands up those of you who have older brothers or sisters. (Hands down) Hands up those of you who have younger brothers or sisters. (Hands down) Hands up those of you who sometimes do not get on well with your brothers or sisters! (Hands down) Hands up those of you who never, ever have rows or fall out with your brothers or sisters! (Hands down) Hands up those of you who are sometimes kept awake at night because younger sisters or brothers cry out for Mummy. (Hands down.)

I wonder if your parents ever have to get cross with you, or your sisters or brothers, at meal times because you are arguing? Meal times, as you well know, can be spoiled because of quarrelling and angry words.

Now, I tell you this, that although some of you may not readily admit the fact, you love your brothers and sisters — even though you may say they are a pain at times, or all the time! Listen to this story, based on a poem called 'The Quarrel'.

David's Truck

Peter was ten and his brother, David, was just four years old. Peter was often upset because his parents seemed to expect him to behave sensibly at all times while David was allowed to get away with murder!

Now Peter loved making small delicate models which he carefully arranged on the shelves in his room. David played with big toys. He had huge, brightly coloured toys including a large truck which he insisted on pushing or pulling all over the house. It was usually loaded with painted wooden bricks which often spilled out when David pulled the truck round corners. One day when Peter arrived home from school he decided to finish making a small model car from a kit he had bought with his pocket money.

When he went to his room he was surprised and angry to find David in there pushing his huge truck around the floor. He was even more angry when he looked down and saw his partly finished small model car crushed by David's truck.

David had knocked against the shelf in Peter's room and the car had fallen in the path of the truck as David dragged it along.

Now the small car was badly damaged.

Peter lost his temper and hit his young brother across the face. 'I hate you and your great stupid truck,' he screamed.

David cried loudly. He rolled on the floor and cried and cried.

At last his tears stopped falling though he continued to cry. With trembling voice he said, 'Peter, you can have my truck to keep instead of your car.'

For some time Peter stood and watched David's shoulders shake in time with his breathless sobbing.

Then, Peter put his arms round his young brother's shoulders.

'I'm sorry I hit you and I didn't mean it when I said I hated you David. I'll try to mend my model,' he said.

'Let me help you,' David pleaded, between sobs.

'All right,' said Peter.

Then they set to work together.

Hymn
Heavenly Father, may thy blessing (*Come and Praise* 62).
I belong to a family, the biggest on earth (*Come and Praise* 69).

CLOSING PRAYER

Let us say together:

May the Lord keep us all in his care; may he watch over those whom we love, and those who love us.

Amen.

Closing music

The pianist plays a few bars of quiet music while all stay still and quiet — to think, reflect or say their own silent prayers.

Any necessary announcements

Recessional music

Suitable music is played by the pianist, group or school orchestra, or from a recording, as the children leave.

For younger children

(For involvement before, during or after assembly.)

- Talk or write about 'My Family'.

- Talk or write about, 'My Sister' or 'My Brother'.

- Draw or paint some 'Family Portraits'.

For older children

(For involvement before, during or after assembly.)

Write a detailed description of your sister or brother. Mention all their good and not-so-good habits and characteristics. Paint a picture of your sister or brother to attach to the written description. (If you do not have a sister or brother, write about your mother or father instead.) Discuss 'Home and Family Life'. Mention the happy and the difficult situations. Make up a short funny play about a boy, a girl and their parents at a typical meal-time scene. Then act out the play. (It should be quite amusing!)

Additional material

Poem
The Quarrel
I quarrelled with my brother,
I don't know what about,
One thing led to another
And somehow we fell out.
The start of it was slight,
The end of it was strong,
He said he was right,
I knew he was wrong!
We hated one another.
The afternoon turned black.
Then suddenly my brother
Thumped me on the back,
And said, 'Oh come along!
We can't go on all night —
I was in the wrong.'
So he was in the right.
Eleanor Farjeon

REMEMBRANCE

Preparation

If poppies are sold in school during the week before Remembrance Sunday, children could be invited to make a contribution in return for poppies and encouraged to wear them for this assembly.

On a table at the front could be placed a simple wooden cross to which poppies are attached. Also on the table could be placed any collection boxes used for the Earl Haig or 'Poppy Fund' money at school.

Alternatively, the cross could be placed on a black cloth strewn with poppies and/or autumn leaves.

Opening music

Appropriate music could be played as the children assemble in silence.

GREETING

Leader: 'Good morning children.'

Children: 'Good morning (leader's name); good morning to all.'
All adults present: 'Good morning children.'

INTRODUCTION

Remembrance Sunday is the nearest Sunday to the 11th of November. On that day we remember and pay tribute to the dead of two world wars. This is our Remembrance Assembly when we too wish to remember all those who died or were injured as a result of war.

PRAYER

Let us pray. We remember in silence those people to whom war has brought sadness and suffering.

(Pause for silent prayer).

O God, help us, together with all children of other nations, as we grow up, to help build a world that shall be free from the evil of war. Lead us daily to think those thoughts, speak those words and do those deeds that will be most helpful in bringing about 'Peace on earth, goodwill towards all,' which is your desire.

Amen.

Hymn
For all the Saints who from their labours rest.
Make me a channel of your peace (*Come and Praise* 147).

Bible reference
True Happiness, St Matthew ch 5 vv 4–9.
Peace, Micah ch 4 v 3.

CONTENT

On Remembrance Sunday wreaths are laid on War Memorials throughout our country and at the Cenotaph in London. You may see pictures of parades and ceremonies on television. In churches and cathedrals during Remembrance Services, a two minutes' silence is observed when people stand and remember those who died during times of war.

During the First World War, many soldiers were killed or were badly injured in a part of Europe called Flanders. It was to help the disabled servicemen that Earl Haig, who fought during the war, suggested that those crippled should make and sell artificial poppies. The money collected should then be used to help those who were disabled as a result of war injuries. Why poppies? Earl Haig remembered that the first wild flowers which grew in the fields of Flanders after the war had been masses of beautiful red poppies.

Here is a lovely story which tells why the poppy was chosen as an emblem of remembrance.

The flowers of remembrance

Before the flowers came to live upon the earth, each one chose where it would grow.

'I shall star the sunny banks,' said the primrose.

'And I shall make the waysides bright,' said the dandelion.

'I shall deck the sweet green fields,' said the daisy.

'And I, the waving meadows,' said the buttercup.

And the tiny violet whispered: 'I shall peep out along the mossy lanes.'

And so, in turn, spoke every lovely flower, until each had chosen its place, except the scarlet poppy.

'I don't know where to grow,' sighed the brightest of all the flowers. 'I love the sun, but I fear the wind and rain, for my petals are fragile and my stem is slender.'

'Come and grow with me,' said the golden corn. 'I will let the sun shine upon you, but I will shelter you from the wind and rain.'

'Thank you golden corn,' said the poppy. 'At last I know where I shall grow.'

So every flower came to live on earth in its chosen place. And they spread and multiplied and filled the earth with their glory.

Then a gentle voice spoke to them and said,

'Little flowers, you have made My world beautiful.'

The flowers heard the voice and grew in gladness. So they would have grown undisturbed, if war had not come to the world and spoiled the beautiful earth. Great stretches of it were laid waste — meadows and cornfields, sunny banks and mossy lanes. The lovely flowers were crushed under trampling feet, until they dared grow no more, but hid themselves deep down in the sheltering ground.

The gentle voice spoke again, but now it was filled with sadness.

'Little flowers,' it said, 'My world is beautiful no more; parts of it are brown and bare, and men, weary with fighting, have forgotten the beauty of My flowers.'

The flowers heard the voice and trembled with sadness, but none dared show its lovely face, none save the scarlet poppy.

'We fear the wind and the rain,' said the poppies, 'and we fear the trampling feet of men; yet we will try to cheer these dreary places, for we are the brightest of all the flowers.' And they pushed their slender stems through the hard, brown earth and spread their lovely blooms about the barren ground. Tired men gazed at them with wonder. 'It is a miracle,' they said.

Winds buffeted the scarlet poppies, rain drenched them and they were crushed by trampling feet, but still, undaunted, they rose and bloomed again to remind men of the beauty of the flowers. The gentle voice spoke again.

'Little poppies,' it said, 'you are the brightest of all My flowers and you are the bravest. Men will remember you for ever.'

And so it has been. For, when the world was at peace once more, men remembered the scarlet poppies that, alone of all the flowers, had spread their glory on the desert places of the earth, and they named them the 'Flowers of Remembrance'. So, to this day, the poppies are the flowers by which all people remember the sadness of war, and pray that it may never come again to take beauty and happiness from the world.

Lilian McCrea, from A Calendar of Stories.

Hymn
I vow to thee, my country.
The National Anthem (Official Peace Version, *Come and Praise* 318).
Peace is flowing like a river (*Come and Praise* 144).

CLOSING READING

'They shall grow not old, as we that are left grow old:
Age shall not weary them, nor the years condemn.
At the going down of the sun and in the morning
We will remember them.'
Laurence Binyon, 'For the Fallen'.

CLOSING PRAYER

Dear God, we pray that you will give peace in our hearts which will help to make peace where we live which will help to make peace in the world.

Amen

Assembly close
(It is suggested that the children leave this Assembly in silence, unaccompanied by any recessional music.)

Further suggestions

● Representative(s) from the local branch of The British Legion could be invited to attend Assembly, carrying their colours.

● Invite a bugler (possibly from a nearby military establishment) to play The Last Post at an appropriate point during Assembly.

● Display a model of The Cenotaph made by older pupils.

● Possible poetry reading: 'The Soldier' by Rupert Brooke.

HANDS

Preparation
If possible, have a copy of the famous picture called *Praying Hands* by Albrecht Durer (1471–1528), to show the children during the Assembly.

Opening music
As the children assemble, music should be played by the school orchestra, a group, soloist or from a recording.

GREETING

Leader: 'Good morning children.'

Children: 'Good morning (leader's name); good morning everyone.'
All adults present: 'Good morning children.'

INTRODUCTION

Look closely at your hands. Move your fingers to make a fist. Open your fingers and see how far it is from the tip of your little finger to the tip of your thumb. This is your hand's span. Use the tips of two fingers to feel your own pulse on your other hand's wrist.

(An adult may need to demonstrate this.)

Can you feel it?

The tips of your fingers are extremely sensitive in order to feel and touch things. I wonder why we have four fingers and one thumb on each hand? I wonder why our fingers are different lengths?

If you had to design a hand, I wonder what it would look like? I believe our present hand design is extremely clever — efficient and complex, yet simple to operate. Let us put our hands together as we say a prayer to thank God for our hands.

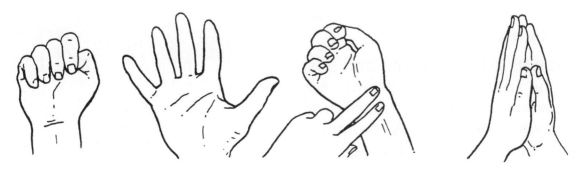

PRAYER

Dear God, we thank you for our hands. Teach us to use them wisely and especially use them to help others.

Amen.

Bible reference
Text 'Whatsoever thy hand findeth to do, do it with thy might.' (Ecclesiastes ch 9 v 10. R.S.V.)
Jesus heals the man with the paralysed hand. (St Mark ch 3 vv 1–6.)

Hymn
Jesus' hands were kind hands.
He gave me eyes so I could see (note verse 3) (*Come and Praise* 18).

CONTENT

(Leader holds up 'Praying Hands' picture).

Look at this famous picture. It is called 'Praying Hands' and this is the story about it. Albrecht, or Albert, and Franz Durer were brothers. They were part of a large German family from Nuremburg. Both Albert and Franz were talented at drawing and painting, just like some of you, and both wished to study to become artists. Albert was taught, initially, by his father and when he was only thirteen he drew a self-portrait which confirmed his great talent. Because the Durer family was quite poor, Albert and Franz could not be given money to train as artists. Then Franz had an idea. He suggested that he should work to earn enough money to pay for his younger brother's training; then, after Albert had completed his studies, they could change over and Franz could train whilst Albert worked.

So it was that Albert trained and became a fine artist, whilst his brother Franz toiled hard to earn the necessary money.

When the time came for the brothers to change roles, Franz said that it was too late for him to train to be an artist. He showed Albert his hard, calloused hands and fingers which had lost their sensitivity. His hands were in such a state because he had worked so hard to pay Albert's tuition fees.

Albert was greatly moved and upset when he saw his loving brother's hands. He vowed to draw a picture of Franz's hands which would show the world 'Hands of Love'. Now, over four hundred

90

years later, many people know the picture 'Praying Hands' by Albrecht Durer. Franz Durer is unknown as an artist, but his hands are famous because of his brother's picture, drawn in gratitude and love.

(Re-told from Sylvia Brimer.)

Hymn
He's got the whole world, in His hand (*Come and Praise* 19).
The wise may bring their learning (*Come and Praise* 64).

CLOSING PRAYER

Let us join together to say,

'May the Lord keep us all in his care; may he watch over those whom we love and those who love us.

Amen'.

Closing music
A very short, quietly played piano interlude.

Close of assembly
After any necessary announcements the children leave whilst appropriate music is played by a pianist, group, orchestra or from a recording.

For younger children
(For involvement before, during or after assembly.)

- Draw round your hand and cut out the silhouette shape. Put your name on your hand shape. (A class 'Hands Frieze' could be made.)

- Measure your hand-span. Measure other objects using your hand-span as a unit of length.

- Make a collection of small objects which you enjoy feeling or stroking.

For older children
(For involvement before, during or after assembly.)

- Make a list of sayings about hands (find out their meanings). Here are some: Many hands make light work. Lend a hand. Hands Up! Hands off! All hands on deck. Second-hand.

- Why do people often shake hands when they meet?

- Draw a very careful, detailed sketch of one of your hands.

- Try out a hand mime to music, e.g. imagine your hands and fingers are flames of a fire which gradually burns more fiercely and eventually dies out completely. (This can be very effective, especially if red and yellow ribbons are attached to your wrists.)

BABIES

Preparation

The following 'props' would be useful for this Assembly:
   i. A simple crib with straw inside it.
   ii. Items that an expectant mother might gather together in preparation for a new baby's arrival. (These items should not be on show at the outset.)

Opening music

Christmas Carols or Advent hymns should be played by soloists, school instrumental group, orchestra or pianist as the children assemble. (Pre-recorded music could be substituted if necessary.)

GREETING

Leader: 'Good morning children.'

Children: 'Good morning (leader's name); good morning everybody.'
All adults present: 'Good morning children.'

INTRODUCTION

Our Assembly today is about Advent.

Advent is the time we remember that Jesus was about to be born. You know that Jesus was born in a stable in Bethlehem because there was no room in the inn.

'Advent tells us Christ is near;

Christmas tells us Christ is here!'

PRAYER

Let us pray:

O God, our loving Father, we are happy and a little excited that Christmas is coming again. Help us to remember that it is first and foremost the birthday of Jesus. Please accept our carols of praise as we look forward to all the happiness, laughter and fun.

Amen.

Hymn

Hark the glad sound!
Jesus, good above all other (*Come and Praise* 23).
Suitable carol of your choice.

Bible reference

The birth of Jesus is announced (St Luke ch 1 vv 30–33).

92

CONTENT

How many of you have younger brothers or sisters? How many of you have a younger brother or sister who is less than one year old? How many of you who have tiny brothers or sisters are kept awake at night because they cry! Do you remember what it was like when your mother was expecting your younger brother or sister? Can you remember what preparations she had to make?

Tell me some of the things you would need to have ready for the arrival of a new baby.

(Suggested items might include: cot, carry-cot, small vest, cardigan, booties, jump-suit, night-clothes, bath, flannel, talcum powder, soap, cream, tiny scissors, feeding bottle, bib, baby-bag, nappies, brush and comb, shampoo, pram or 'buggy' etc. As the names of the items are called out, if you have them available, put them on show — or ask individual children to come out and hold them. Alternatively, as the names are called out, a list could be written up — though this is not as effective.)

Can you imagine Mary carrying all these items with her, on the donkey's back! Now look at what Mary had when Jesus was born.

(Show the crib and ask the children to contrast the simple crib and straw with all the items that are often available for a child born nowadays. Let the children spend a few moments contemplating the difference. It is effective if the crib is placed away from the modern items.)

PRAYER

O God in heaven, we thank you for all the babies we know and love. Especially today we thank you for sending the baby Jesus to Mary on the first Christmas.

Amen.

(The Lord's Prayer, if desired).

Hymn
Christmas is coming, is coming again.
O come, O come, Emmanuel!
Other suitable carol of your choice.

CLOSING PRAYER

We say together

May the Lord keep us all in his care. May he watch over those whom we love, and those who love us.

Amen.

Closing music
Quiet, very short piece of music is played by the pianist.

Recessional music
Children leave Assembly (after any necessary announcements),
whilst appropriate music is played.

For younger children
(For involvement before, during or after assembly.)

- Draw a picture of your young brother or sister — or of any baby. Write or tell about him/her.

- Draw pictures of some of the things you would need for a new baby.

- Bring in photographs of yourself when you were a baby.

- Consider making and/or using an Advent Calendar.

For older children
(For involvement before, during or after assembly.)

- How do some animals prepare for their babies?

- Find out about a young baby's development. (Refer, if possible, to a Baby Book that has been completed.)

- What safety precautions do parents need to take in order to protect their babies?

- What is an Advent Ring?

- Find out what the five candles on an Advent ring represent.

Further suggestions

- Consider the possibility of inviting either an expectant mother or a mother with a very young baby to Assembly — to tell about how to prepare for a baby's arrival, and to answer any questions the children may have.

- Undertake a class project on 'Babies'.

(There are obviously possible links here with Sex Education if desired.)

SADNESS

This assembly needs to be handled with sensitivity, careful thought and careful planning.

Opening music
Appropriate music should be selected and played by a pianist, group, school orchestra or from a recording as all assemble.

GREETING

Leader: 'Good morning children.'

Children: 'Good morning (leader's name); good morning to all.'
All adults present: 'Good morning children.'

INTRODUCTION

Life is not always happy, bright and joyful. Sometimes we pass through sad and difficult times.

When someone we love dearly is seriously ill or dies, we naturally experience great sorrow — but we can gain strength and comfort from the knowledge that Jesus shares our grief and will give us strength to face all the distress and sadness.

PRAYER

O God, Creator of Life, help us to remember that we are never alone and that you are always by our side. Teach us how to trust you, always; to be brave in times of sadness and to fear nothing. Help us to find the sunshine even among the shadows of difficult times.

Amen.

The Lord's Prayer (if desired).

Bible reference
Psalm 23.
Psalm 56 vv 3–4 .
Jesus the Way to the Father, St John ch 14 vv 1–6.

Hymn
Jesus, Friend of little children.
From the darkness came light (*Come and Praise* 29).

CONTENT

No doubt all of you have been upset at some time or other, because of the death of somebody you have loved. Perhaps you have faced great sadness when a pet has died. Life can sometimes be very difficult and hard. Today's story is a sad one and it may even remind you of a sad time or times in your life.

The Gardening Club

The Headteacher announced in assembly that a Gardening Club would be started in school.

Members of the club would meet weekly in the greenhouse that had been provided by the School Friends' Association.

Many of the children were excited and looked forward to the first session of the new club which was fixed for after school on the following Wednesday.

'The club will be run by Mr Tony Brown who is a retired teacher,' said the Headteacher, 'and he will be willing to give advice on growing all kinds of flowers and plants.'

Michael was particularly thrilled. He was ten years old and for two years he had grown things in his own small garden which had been given to him by his parents. Michael was one of the first to join the new club and quickly became one of its keenest members.

Every Wednesday after school Michael raced to the greenhouse to meet Mr Brown, who was a kind, friendly man who knew a great deal about growing things. Michael planted seeds and bulbs and took cuttings. He spent many hours watering and tending his plants under the watchful eye of Mr Brown.

For nearly two years Michael went to the club which met throughout the year. Michael noticed that sometimes Mr Brown seemed tired and breathless, especially if he bent down for long. His hair was white; his voice was crackly and his fingers often trembled when he held tiny seedlings that needed transplanting.

Mr Brown was as enthusiastic as Michael about gardening. He always enjoyed seeing the lovely flowers that had been grown by the gardening club members. He enjoyed being with the children who had all grown to love him.

One Wednesday, the Headteacher called the children together and told them that their dear friend, Mr Brown, had died suddenly the previous evening.

Michael decided to go to the greenhouse, as usual, after school. On the bench was a large cardboard box. Attached to the box was a note. Michael read the message on the note which simply said, 'The small trowel, small fork, secateurs and gardening gloves are for use by Gardening Club members'. The note was signed by Mrs Brown.

Michael stood for some moments and stared sadly at the contents of the box and his eyes filled with tears. He could not swallow easily and he did not feel like staying there. He turned to go but then caught sight of the trays of seeds that he and Mr Brown had planted two weeks before. He quietly filled his watering can and watered the seeds because he knew that is what Mr Brown would have wished him to do.

Then Michael walked slowly and sadly home.

Hymn
God who made the earth (*Come and Praise* 10).
Can you be sure that the rain will fall? (*Come and Praise* 31).

CLOSING PRAYER

Let us say together:

May the Lord keep us all in his care; may he watch over those whom we love, and those who love us.

Amen.

Closing music
The pianist plays a few bars of quiet music whilst all present remain still in silent contemplation.
Any necessary announcements.

Recessional music
Suitable music is played by the pianist, group, school orchestra or from a recording as all leave the assembly.

For younger children
(For involvement before, during or after assembly.)

- Children are invited to tell about their sad experiences.

- Children are invited to tell about sad stories they have read or heard.

- Children are invited to make up and act out a sad play.

For older children
(For involvement before, during or after assembly.)

- Children are invited to write or tell about their own personal sad experiences.

- Children are invited to write or tell about sad stories they have read or sad films or plays that they have seen.

- Class discussion: sadness, grief, suffering, tears, death, sorrow, etc.

- Consider the effects of grief and how comfort can be given.

- How should one react when meeting people who are grieving?

SKILLED HANDS

Opening music
Music, by a pianist, group of children, school orchestra or from a recording is played as the children enter quietly and take their places.

GREETING

Leader: 'Good morning children.'

Children: 'Good morning (leader's name); good morning to everyone.'
All adults present: 'Good morning children.'

INTRODUCTION

In our Assembly today we will hear about a boy who had great talent and who, when he grew up, used his skill to create beautiful things.

Different people have different skills and abilities. Have you discovered yet what you are good at? No doubt you know who is a fast runner in your class. Do you know who is the fastest swimmer in your class? Could you say who, in your class, is good at mathematics, or writing, or drawing, or making things? Some children seem to be good at everything they do! Some children feel that they are not good at doing anything but, in time, they will discover that they have talent and they will achieve success.

Remember one thing — whatever you find yourself doing, do it the very best that you can!

Bible reference
'Whatsoever thy hand findeth to do, do it with thy might'.
Ecclesiastes, ch 9, v 10 (Authorised Version).

Hymn
Jesus' hands were kind hands.
God who made the earth (*Come and Praise* 10).

PRAYER

Dear God, help us to use our minds to think wisely, and our hands to work skilfully. Help us to discover the things we can do really well. If and when we find new skills difficult to learn, help us to persevere and always try our best. Save us from ever boasting about our cleverness or talent but keep us humble and thankful to you for giving us skill. May we never make fun of people who find learning difficult and let us never tease clumsy people.

Amen.

The Lord's Prayer (if desired).

CONTENT

This is a story told about an Italian boy named Antonio Canova.

Thomasso, the head cook at Senator Giovanni's castle, was a worried man. He had been asked by his master to produce a table-centre decoration for a grand banquet. On previous occasions Thomasso had made castles and dragons in pastry, birds out of sugar and a clock made of sweets. Now he could not think of anything new. He had run out of ideas!

He told his cousin about his worry. His cousin's ten year old son, whose name was Antonio, heard the two men discussing the problem.

'Let me try to help,' pleaded the boy. 'I know that I could make something really special.'

'What could you possibly create? You're only a ten year old boy,' said Thomasso.

At last, after much discussion and in desperation, Thomasso agreed to let the boy try out his idea.

The boy, Antonio, asked for a large block of butter and a small room in which he could work undisturbed.

Antonio loved modelling in clay and he set to work, carefully carving and shaping the butter. For twelve hours he worked and, gradually, he changed the shapeless lump of butter into a beautiful crouching lion.

The animal was perfect in every detail. Even though it was only a table decoration which would not last, Antonio made his model as well as he possibly could. Thomasso and Senator Giovanni Falier were thrilled and delighted when they saw Antonio's crouching lion. The Senator sent for Antonio and congratulated him. Later, Senator Giovanni arranged for Antonio to receive instruction from the finest sculptors in Italy and he paid all fees and expenses.

Antonio Canova (1757–1822), the peasant boy, became a great and famous sculptor and his carvings and works are world famous today.

(Re-told from Sylvia Brimer.)

Hymn
The wise may bring their learning (*Come and Praise* 64).
I will bring to you the best gift I can offer (*Come and Praise* 59).

CLOSING PRAYER

Let us say together:

May the Lord keep us all in his care; may he watch over those whom we love and those who love us.

Amen.

Closing music
A very short, quietly played piano piece.
Any necessary announcements.

Recessional music
The children leave, accompanied by appropriate music.

For younger children
(For involvement before, during or after assembly.)

- Make and show a model animal using clay, play-doh or similar material.

- Make and show an 'animal-made-from-vegetable' model.

- Make a jelly mould crouching rabbit or similar and look at its detail.

For older children
(For involvement before, during or after assembly.)

- Carve an animal from a solid lump of hard clay, soft brick, soft wood, block salt (or similar material), using tools carefully, under supervision. (This is difficult — but worthwhile.) Show your model.

- Create a model animal from a lump of soft clay.

- Make a papier-mache animal model.

- Show pictures of some of Antonio Canova's famous sculptures (e.g. The Three Graces).

WINTER

Preparation
If possible have a small vase of snowdrops on view.

Opening music
Appropriate music is played by a pianist, group, school orchestra or from a recording as children enter and take their places, quietly.

GREETING

Leader: 'Good morning children.'

Children: 'Good morning (leader's name); good morning to all.'
All adults present: 'Good morning children.'

INTRODUCTION

There are so many different kinds of weather. I am sure that you know the four seasons and could tell about the joys that each one brings. What do you like about winter?

(Answers may include: snow, frost patterns, Christmas, sliding, tobogganing, skiing, sleighing, snowballing, warm evenings indoors, etc.)

Winter can be beautiful. Frosted trees or snow covered countryside in winter sunshine can be breathtaking to view. Let us say a prayer about wintertime.

PRAYER

We thank you God for the beauties and blessings of winter. We thank you for the loveliness of bare branches and for sparkling frost and icicles; for the resting time for plants and animals; for snow which gives us winter fun — for snowmen, snowballs, slides and sledges. We thank you too for the warmth of our homes, thick coats and warm cosy beds. Finally we thank you for snowdrops, bringing us your message of the promise of spring.

Amen.

The Lord's Prayer (if desired).

Hymn
I will bring to you the best gift I can offer (*Come and Praise* 59).
To God who makes all lovely things.

Bible reference
God's power over storms, Job ch 37 vv 3, 5–6, 9–10.
(From the Apocrypha) Ecclesiasticus ch 43 vv 13-20.
Psalm 147 vv 15–18.

CONTENT

The first snowdrops flower in January.

(Show the snowdrops, if available, and explain that there are many different varieties.)

They are one of the earliest flowers to blossom in the New Year. Snowdrops are not white, as many people imagine. They are green and white (as you can see).

We welcome the lovely snowdrops with their drooping heads because we know they bloom as a promise of the coming of spring. Our story today is about snowdrops.

The Legend of the First Snowdrops

After Adam and Eve had disobeyed God by eating the forbidden fruit, they had to leave the Garden of Eden. It was bitterly cold as they made their way out of the beautiful garden into a lonely wilderness where no flowers blossomed and no birds sang.

God took pity on them and sent a guardian angel to watch over them.

Slowly Adam and Eve wandered, seeking shelter. As they walked, Eve's tears of sadness fell and mingled with the soft falling snow. The angel turned both tears and snowflakes into beautiful white and green snowdrops — the first snowdrops that ever appeared on the earth. Then the angel said that the snowdrops would return every year as a promise that God is never angry for ever, and his love, like the springtime, will always come to us just as the springtime follows even the hardest of winters.

Hymn
Fill your hearts with joy and gladness (*Come and Praise* 9).
Lay my white cloak on the ground (*Come and Praise* 112).

Closing music
A quiet, very short piece of music is played by the pianist.
Any necessary announcements.

Recessional music
Children leave the assembly accompanied by music played by a pianist, group, school orchestra or from a recording.

For younger children
(For involvement before, during or after assembly.)

- Discuss 'The Seasons' and/or 'The Months' and relate to weather changes.
- Read poems about winter.
- Compose poems about winter. (Use WINTER as an acrostic.)
- Find out about hibernation, and which animals hibernate.
- Use a 'Winter' mural on which to stick cut-out pictures or silhouettes by the children, depicting aspects of the season.

For older children
(For involvement before, during or after assembly.)

- Using appropriate music, make up a winter dance/drama. Use spiky movements (using fingers especially) to reflect frost (Jack Frost). Slower music and graceful, 'dying' movement can be used to interpret snow falling etc.
- Experiment to see how long ice takes to melt.
- If possible, examine snowflakes before they melt. (Use a magnifying glass.) Are all snowflakes different? Do they have symmetrical shapes?
- Find and recite poems about Winter or the seasons or the months.

Additional material
January is named after the god Janus. It was made the first month of the year by Julius Caesar when he reformed the calendar in 45 BC. The Roman Temple of Janus had twelve windows — one for each month, and four doors — one for each season.

Finger mime
This is how snowflakes play about,
Up in cloudland they dance in and out.
This is how snowflakes whirl down the street,
Powdering everyone white that they meet.
This is how snowflakes cover the trees,
Branches and twigs then bend in the breeze ...
This is how snowflakes cover the ground,
— Cover it quickly, with never a sound.
This is how people shiver and shake
On a snowy-white morning when first they awake.
This is how snowflakes melt away
When the sun sends out his beams to play.
(from Sing Praises)

Poem
The North Wind

The north wind doth blow,
And we shall have snow,
And what will poor robin do then, poor thing?
O, he'll go to the barn,
And to keep himself warm,
He'll hide his head under his wing, poor thing.

The north wind doth blow,
And we shall have snow,
And what will the children do then, poor things?
O, when lessons are done,
They'll jump, skip and run,
And play till they make themselves warm, poor things!
(from Sing Praises)